MW01170034

A Dream To Sell

An Autobiography by Plato S. Wilson

ISBN: 0-9729970-0-8

First Printing March 2003

Published by:
Madison Advertising & Publishing Services, Inc.
2132 Fordem Avenue
Madison, Wisconsin 53704

Manufactured in the United States of America

This book is my
personal remembrance of the
material that I have written,
having lived and experienced the
events and being intimately close
to all principals involved.
The book is not a precise
historical documentary.

ACKNOWLEDGEMENTS

My good friend and fabulous merchant upon whom I called on for years, Boyce Grindstaff, had always encouraged me and tried to motivate me to write my life story in the "Golden Years" (1946-1990) in the Home Furnishings Industry. His efforts finally culminated in March, 2002, during a Caribbean cruise our families shared. He extracted a promise from me to become serious about producing an autobiography. There were many others along the way who encouraged me to "put it down on paper." I sincerely thank Boyce and the others who believed I was capable and had a story to tell.

The main motivation, however, came from my wife, Dixie, who sat me down to a table and chair, paper, pen and a dictionary and insisted that I write this book. We had just arrived at our summer cottage at Gingercake, and it was June 1, 2002. She never let up on the pressure until, four months later, the book was complete. I used her every day as I wrote, for spelling, grammar and proof-reading. She never ever hesitated to help me with any request. I am forever indebted to her for her patience and vital help, and especially for giving up her husband of four years for four months that we could have done many other exiting activities together. She is a trooper!

I want to thank again, most sincerely, my loyal typist Anita Watson who works at Lees-McRae College in the Planned Giving office. During her time off in the evenings and weekends, she labored at the difficult task of trying to read my poor handwriting and typing it in an orderly form. Her patience with my corrections and re-writes were beyond the call of duty. Each time, Anita would just flash that unique smile and re-double her effort. Thank you, yet another time, Anita, for your great help.

Thanks also go to our daughter, Susan, who encouraged and

helped me with details of our family life. She probably is surprised that I actually had the patience to sit down and write my life's story and actually finish it.

I am, indeed, privileged to have my dear friend and former boss Carlton Mallory, Vice President of Henkel Harris, write the introduction to this book. He is most respected in the furniture industry for his devotion to quality manufacturing and his unexcelled integrity. Carlton was a dream person to work with for the last wonderful, and most rewarding, eight years of my forty-four year career. Whether I deserve his extravagant remarks I do not know, but I just wish my dear mother were alive to read her son's introduction written by Carlton Mallory, a giant in the furniture industry! Thank you, sincerely, Carlton, for your most generous remarks!

I am very deeply indebted for the professional help and inspiration of my long time friend and fellow salesman while I worked for Henredon Furniture Industries, David Christensen, my publisher who lives in Madison, WI and heads his distinguished company – Madison Advertising and Publishing Services with his wife, Vicki. David guided me, an amateur, through the publishing art, finally getting it in acceptable form and actually publishing the book, digitally. Without his great help and his professional staff, this book would not have happened. Thanks to all there!

Lastly, and most certainly not least, I am thankful for the keen eyes and professional abilities of my long-time friend Joe E. Brown, the retired editor of our High Point Enterprise newspaper. He had a mammoth task of editing my humble effort of writing this book. He spent much time and expert attention in making the book presentable to our readers. I sincerely thank Joe for his extra efforts.

*I dedicate this book to all the
people who have shaped my life
and especially to my wife, Dixie,
for her grace and beauty, who
motivated and helped me
to write this book, and to
daughter Susan for her
love and compassion.*

Table of Contents

INTRODUCTION

By the time I first met Plato Wilson in September of 1981, he was already a legend. Known far and wide for his sales success with Henredon, he was both admired and envied. Even in the midst of territorial reductions, his sales volume consistently increased because he simply sold more furniture than anyone thought imaginable.

Communicating, motivating, and selling are intuitive to Plato. These qualities, together with his ambitious nature, intensity and determination, make him a forceful presence. In fact, when I compare Plato to the many other outstanding salesmen I have known, I realize right away that Plato exists on a plateau of his own. I believe it is his unique ability to empower and inspire people that sets him apart. And Plato does not reserve this inspirational enthusiasm just for the key players in a deal. His particular brand of selling excludes no one. He treats everyone — from the warehouse and delivery personnel to the sales and design teams — with the same dignity and respect. Throughout Plato's career, these are the kinds of extra efforts for which he has been handsomely rewarded.

Timing and circumstances within the interior furnishings industry combined to provide Plato with a series of opportunities, the likes of which we may never see again. Simply stated, this was an era when entrepreneurialism was both appreciated and supported, and individual initiative, which Plato Wilson possessed in abundance, was encouraged to the fullest extent. But, for reasons of their own, Henredon and Plato Wilson — the man, the legend, the modern-day selling machine — decided to bring to an end their long and prosperous journey together. The impact of this decision must be regarded in light of the fact that by this time in his career, Plato Wilson's name and reputation were known by furniture retailers and manufacturers not only in North Carolina but throughout the continental United States.

About this same time, Henkel Harris was looking for someone to represent the company in the states of North and South Carolina. Among a number of other impressive names to express interest in this opportunity was Plato Wilson. I was not only amazed but also curiously interested in why our small company, with limited production capacity by design, would be attractive to this legendary and powerful individual. Cautiously, I decided to speak with him. Given his relentless sales pace, I was literally afraid that he could overwhelm our factory with the sheer number of orders he would write.

To my surprise, however, I found that Plato had, in a very insightful way and for reasons completely acceptable to him and his family, reordered his priorities. He wished to end his career with a company where his contribution could be significant and his work respected with lasting value. To our good fortune, Plato decided that Henkel Harris was just that company and accepted my offer to join our sales force. To his credit, and at an age and level of success where one does not easily change attitudes or habits, Plato Wilson did so with distinction and style, again demonstrating his exceptional adaptability. For over eight years until his retirement in 1989, Plato Wilson sold our furniture with that same innate passion and enthusiasm that will always make him legendary in the furniture industry.

If anyone is qualified to write about a life in sales, it is Plato Wilson, especially because Plato did not leave "life" behind while doggedly chasing a sale. There is an incredible sense of balance in the choices he has made. He learned the lessons of family early on, obtained a solid education, and served his country in the South Pacific during World War II. Beyond family and selling, his other passion is Duke University, his alma mater, which he has also very generously remembered. Plato apprenticed with some of the brightest visionaries in our industry and then went on to realize the full measure of his potential as the consummate salesman of his time.

Carlton Mallory
Vice President
Henkel-Harris Furniture Co.

CHAPTER 1

Growing Up

9/30/89
Mr. Carlton Mallory, VP
Henkel-Harris Furn.
P.O. Box 217
Winchester, VA 22601

Dear Carlton:

After 44 years, 2.6 million miles traveled, 28 autos worn out, five furniture companies, life sales of $154,100,000 — all in the search of The Holy Grail — the order; I want to announce that I have had a ball each and every day of my career. I have especially enjoyed the past eight years with HENKEL-HARRIS — my best furniture line!

I am deeply indebted to the thousands of excellent and dedicated craftsmen and management people for making my life so exciting and rewarding. I could not have chosen a profession that I would have enjoyed more. On the other side, I have had the very best retail stores and retail people to share my life. They made the ultimate sales that made us all look so successful. Without all of you, I would have not achieved my goals. Thanks to all of you for making a simple job into a career for me.

I have also been privileged to work with some of the best and most professional road salesmen in the industry. I owe much of my meager success to their help and encouragement. And to the great service people back at the factories, I just want to say that you made me appear much more professional than I would have been were you not behind me each day. To the owners of the factories and to the retail entrepreneurs, my thanks for your venture capital and wisdom that gave to me the opportunity to use my ever-growing ambition to be a professional salesman, I salute all of you!

As was the case when I broke into this industry, I now think it is time for me to retire and make room for another aspiring younger man to have his "time at bat." I would like to give to you, Carlton, my retirement notice effective 12/31/89. I truly believe my last eight years with Henkel-Harris have been my happiest and most rewarding of my long career. I thank you, sincerely, for the great opportunity you gave to me. I will miss each and every one of you at Henkel-Harris and will fondly remember you for being "just possibly... America's finest furniture makers"! Here's to your future prosperity and good fortune. If I can ever be of any service to you, please let me know.

Thanks for everything!

Most sincerely,
Plato S. Wilson
908 Parkwood Cir.
High Point, N.C. 27260

*E*ven today, as I begin to write, at the urging of many friends, about my life and career, I am shocked to know that my life, with all its twists and turns, would put me in the position to write the letter that ended my professional career. I could not, in my fondest dreams, have guessed my entire business life would have been in the home furnishings industry. As it turned out, my career has been in what has been called the "Golden Years" in the American furniture manufactory business. A rare time, indeed!

In retrospect, I now know that one's life is shaped and molded by the people with whom one comes into contact and by the opportunities recognized and the passion expended to maximize his or her possibilities. No person is an island.

It was in the middle of the "Roaring Twenties," four years before the great financial "Crash of 1929," that I was born, a son and last child to Mabel and Albert Wilson in Morganton, NC. The date was November 1, 1925. Jazz was king, and the women rolled their stockings and wore "headache bands." It was a pretty good time to be born. But, as my parents and their generation soon found out, "what goes up will come down!" The "Crash of Twenty-Nine" leveled almost everyone. All they had left was each other and families to try to support.

My first memories were of living in a big house in downtown Morganton that my father had rented for twenty-five dollars a month and then sublet rooms to four other couples for six dollars a month each. In essence, it was a commune long before the word was used. So I had five mothers and five daddies! We never knew what we would be eating for the next meal until everyone came home with something to cook. One might think this was a gloomy situation, but in contrast, happiness abounded. We had everything but money.

A Dream to Sell

Friends said of my father that he was very astute in that he saw the crash coming in 1927 and went broke then so he could get some experience at being poor. He managed to bankrupt a small chain of barber shops that he had inherited from his father, John Wilson. The truth was that he had let drinking whisky do him in. Later my father, with the help of his brother Harry, was able to get a job at the post office as a custodian. It took the help of a U.S. senator (Bob Reynolds) to obtain this lowly job. That's how tough times were at this point on the calendar. Dad later became a city mail carrier and still later, a rural mail carrier. My father only attended the sixth grade in a one-room schoolhouse. In that class there were pupils who were later to become U.S. senators: Sam Ervin II and Everett Jordan! My uncle Harry L. Wilson Sr., for whom I would later work, dropped out of the fourth grade to go to work for the Lazarus brothers who had come to Morganton from Baltimore. They were "class people" who promised my uncle that if he would drop out of school and let them teach him the business, at their death they would give it to him. He did and led that great ladies' and gentlemen's department store successfully, into more than 100 years.

Later, our family acquired my great grandmother's home and remodeled it. It sat on a big lot. We set it up as an "in-town farm" where we took care of my Uncle Harry's four pure-bred Guernsey milk cows. I was in business at eight years of age: I milked the cows, Mother processed the milk into bottles, churned the milk for buttermilk and butter, and then I delivered all products before school. This was the hottest job in the summer and the coldest in the winter. In addition, I was selling the compost from the cows to the best families in town. This last "business" came after my older sister Rosa Lee gave me a $20 pony for Christmas. I also saw the need to haul off leaves that people raked in their yards. I would make compost out of the leaves and haul it back to the same people who had paid me originally to haul them off! I collected both ways and didn't have any material cost. I also plowed gardens. I was making money! We later became share croppers by growing corn and hay on other peoples' farms out in the country. The owners supplied the land, mules and the seeds. We furnished the labor. We received 50 percent of the crop. At this time I was about 12 years old. I took a part-time job (afternoons after school and all day Saturdays) with Uncle Harry at Lazarus Department Store. He paid me 20 cents per afternoon (3-8 p.m.) and 50 cents for all day Saturday. I unpacked clothing, ran errands, swept out the store and then walked and delivered packages. I was also learning the retail clothing business!

Because of my father's drinking problem and our resulting poverty, I was turning into an introvert. The name Plato didn't help the situation, either. I did not like what was happening to me. One day I asked myself, "If we had the money to go to a psychologist, what advice would I receive?" I answered the question — from common sense: "Make yourself face the public!" I did and got into every play that came to the school. I joined the debating team and clubs. As a result, I became an extrovert. I was elected business manager of our Morganton High School's first yearbook. In selling ads for the yearbook, I met T. Henry Wilson, president of Drexel Furniture Company. It had just been published in a state newspaper that he was the highest paid man in North Carolina in the year 1939. He earned $125,000 that year — not a bad man to know!

Launching my high school advertising campaign, I first went to my uncle Harry for whom I worked at the time (I was 15 years old). I knew that he was very tight and his reaction to the request that he buy a half-page ad for $37.50 was no big surprise. He said that I first should call on Henry Wilson (no relation), president of nearby Drexel Furniture Company in Drexel, NC. Uncle Harry said that he would buy half of what Henry bought, knowing Henry would not buy anything! I called and made an appointment with Mr. Wilson, and I arranged for my mother to drive me there for the appointment. I nervously walked into this huge mahogany paneled office to see Mr. Wilson for the first time. He greeted me warmly and asked what I had on my mind. I told him that I was the business manager of Morganton High School's first yearbook and that I had reserved the front page ad of the annual for Drexel Furniture Company. He went on to say that Drexel Furniture did not buy local advertisements but spent their ad money on national ads in "shelter magazines."

He sat down and began to open his mail. Evidently, the appointment was over.

Somehow, I had the audacity to utter, "But, Mr. Wilson, you are making the mistake of your life!"

He looked up at me and said, "How's that?"

I said, "Mr. Wilson, don't you know that the source of all your labor — craftsmen, secretaries, foremen, and management — comes from this high school? How would you like to be one of these that will give their life to your company and not even see an ad in their yearbook?"

He said, "I believe that I have made a mistake. Can I buy two pages?"

I said, "I think I can arrange for you to do so!"

At this point my mind went back to my uncle who would now have to buy a whole page — a total sale of three pages! I thanked him and turned to go out the door. I was 16 feet tall as I placed my hand on the doorknob to exit. Then I heard him say, "Wait a minute! I want you to sell furniture for me."

Since I was on a roll, I said, "When?"

He said, "Oh, when the war (WWII) is over and you are educated."

"You bet."

I left his office thinking about all those big cars that salesmen drove when they visited Morganton and worked for Drexel Furniture Company. I wanted that life. In 1943 I graduated from Morganton High School and was soon to be inducted into the army. I carried my dream with me all through the war — that of working for the most outstanding (Davidson College graduate, Harvard MBA) educated man I ever heard of.

In the summer of 1942, I was employed by our neighbor, Mr. Jim Harbinson, a land surveyor, to help survey and lay out a vital defense plant in Morganton to manufacture carbon by the Great Lakes Carbon Company. I really felt that I was helping with the war effort. That same summer, we surveyed and laid out an emergency air field between Morganton and Lenoir, to be used by the U.S. Air Force. This airfield later became the Morganton-Lenoir Airport.

After I recovered from my period of being an introvert, my high school days were filled with fun. An anonymous lady in town made a gift to me of free dance lessons with Carl Morgan and his wife. What a gift! I was to go on and enjoy those lessons for the rest of my life. People are wonderful! I developed many lifelong friends during my high school days. Much to my surprise, when the superlatives were voted on during senior year 1943, I was voted to be Wittiest, Best All Around and Best Personality.

Some of my best friends in Morganton High School were Harold Mitchell, Bill Connelly, Penn Hyams, Frank Patton, Bill Carter, Gene Harrell, Sam Ervin III, John Collett, Charles Vernon and Charles Kistler. There were others; however, the aforementioned friends were for life. True friends are hard to come by!

After graduation, I registered for the service draft. While waiting to be called, I went to work full time for my Uncle Harry at Lazarus Department Store as a full-fledged salesman. I bought a 1929 A-Model Ford two-seated convertible car — for $50.00! I was mobile! I had one fantastic summer and early fall while dating all the good looking girls in our area.

Finally I was drafted in the fall of 1943 and was sent to Fort Bragg, NC, for assignment. I was assigned to the 120th General Hospital then training at Camp Van Dorn in Centerville, MS. After three months of rigorous basic training we were granted a 10-day leave before shipping overseas. Fun prevailed in the twenty-hour days before I reported back to Camp Van Dorn. We were issued winter gear and shipped to Oakland, CA for debarkation overseas. We just knew that we were going to Alaska! Well, guess what, with all of our winter gear (overcoats and all) we set sail for the Southwest Pacific! This took 29 days at sea because we were unescorted and had to zig-zag for safety purposes. We landed in New Guinea in time for us to take care of the casualties from the major battle of Buna. We moved up the coast of New Guinea, sometimes breaking up into surgical teams (MASH Units) for special operations. Later we arrived in the Philippines and finally in the city of Manila where we occupied San Thomas University for our hospital. However, reaching Manila was a very circuitous journey. Captain William C. Drew, a former dentist from Georgia, and I were sent as an advanced party on the hospital ship *Emily H. Weeder* to select a hospital site in Baguio, northern Luzon in the Philippine Islands. The date was early March, 1945. We arrived at Lingayen Gulf to find the whole gulf area under fire by the Japanese. Our ship promptly sailed back out into the China Sea until we were given orders to sail to Manila Bay, stopping at Corregidor Island at the entrance to Manila Bay to up load critically wounded soldiers to our hospital ship. We then proceeded into the bay, among hundreds of sunken ships, to be down loaded at a make shift dock. The battle was in full fury within Manila's Walled City section. I finally found Captain Drew, albeit in a drunken condition. He told me to take over the search for our hospital site. I spoke with a sergeant at the port side of the city and asked him for suggestions for our site. His combat company had passed by a golf course on the near north side of the city and he suggested that this could be a place for us because the long fairways would allow small planes to bring in the wounded. I commandeered a jeep and proceeded to locate the golf course named "Wac Wac" (pronounced "walk walk"). I thought to myself that this was the most appropriately named golf course that I had ever heard. I finally found it and it appeared perfect. I requested the use of the facility and was granted permission for its use by our hospital. I then went back to the docks to try and locate Captain Drew to report my good news. It took a whole day, but I found him and he cabled our commanding officer back in Finschhafen, New Guinea, our success on finding a proper site. I worked at a medical aid station in Manila for about two weeks while we awaited the arrival of our 120th General Hospital made up of 75 officers and 500 enlisted men. As we began to set up our huge hospital, something very surprising happened! We discovered that as we tried to drive in the wooden stakes they were breaking off, and as a result, we could not erect the tents. We realized, shortly, that in the construction of the golf course, only a small amount of top soil had been placed over hard coral rocks. Our Colonel Smith, commander, sought me out and read me the riot act for not having checked this problem out sufficiently. He finally patted me on the back and said that he would have probably made the same mistake. Within days, we moved our hospital to the San Thomas University which had hosted all American internees during the occupation by the Japanese. Most of the 75 that had survived this occupation were in pathetic condition and were skin and bones, weighing less than 60 pounds. So our first patients were these unfortunate people. We fed them very small portions of food six or eight times a day and gave them the proper medication. After approximately two weeks, we boarded them on planes bound for the U.S. where the slow process of regaining their health would take place. They, in time, would become well. In the telling of this episode of our roundabout trip to Manila, it reminded me that I had learned a life's lesson: Always be thorough when given responsibility.

Mixed in with the tense and serious side of fighting a war in the South Pacific, there were lighter times that allowed for humor and relaxation. One of these times is revealed in the following story: At that time our mobile hospital was set up in the New Guinea area. We 500 enlisted men were called on to build an officers' club for our many doctors and command officers. The site they chose was a most beautiful one situated on a high coral bluff overlooking the ocean. We did not have our hearts in the project, to say the least, in that it would be "off limits" for us, and we were not allowed to have a club for ourselves. However, we completed the beautiful club and then were asked to obtain palm fronds by climbing the 100-foot palm trees in the area. These were used to construct a tall fence around the entire club area so that we enlisted men could not see all the fun that the officers and our female nurses were having. One can imagine the resentment we had over the project. Well, the club and fence were completed, and on opening night a big party was scheduled. Somehow, about midnight, the fence was set afire, no doubt by some enlisted men, and the huge fire broke up the happy party. Luckily no one was injured, but we were not asked to rebuild the fence. Our officers were much nicer to us from that incident onward. Sometimes, one has to gain the attention of others.

Another interesting light story that I was involved in while we were in New Guinea was that of "bootlegging" whisky. In a combat zone, each soldier was entitled to buy one can of beer per day. Our commander thought this was too much trouble, so he simplified the rule by accumulating a month's supply and issued a whole case (twenty-four cans) once a month. This resulted in a beer bash that was distasteful to many of our men who did not drink at all, including me. There was a large detachment of Australian troops near our camp that loved beer but did not care for their abundant supply of whisky that was brought up often from Australia. I clearly saw an opportunity to make some easy money. I would purchase the beer allotments from our non-drinkers on the grounds, and that would eliminate a lot of the beer from our camp. I then transported the beer over to the "Diggers" (Australian soldiers) to trade for their whisky. I then brought back the whisky to our camp and sold it for two or three times its value. In the process, I made a handsome profit, which I sent home to my mother to enable her to live more comfortably. I was "bootlegging" but at the same time I was helping my mom. Money was of no value living in the jungle. It was a win-win situation in that everyone seemed happy. Entrepreneurial genes are sometimes hard to suppress!

As we were getting ready to sail for Japan, the atomic bomb was dropped. Relief was experienced by us all. By this time I was the sergeant major of our unit, since our senior staffers were being rotated back home. I was given orders to deactivate our entire hospital and give all of our vast medical supplies and equipment to the University. I made the final morning report which transferred me out, and I reported to a replacement depot for my return to the U.S. by ship transport. We finally reached San Francisco in January 1946. They told us that we could have anything we desired for a dream dinner, regardless of the arrival, day or night. Well, we did and what a meal that was, all served by white-dressed German prisoners of war. Our arrival time was 2 a.m.! I still remember those steaks and fresh eggs and milkshakes — all of which we had not tasted in almost three years. What a treat! Immediately after that dinner, I telephoned my mother and dad to tell them that I had made it back unharmed, and I would soon be home. None of us could talk much due to the sobs of joy. The Lord had brought me home and we all thanked Him!

On a very cold and snowy night at midnight, I finally arrived home from the South Pacific to see my family and Mr. T. Henry Wilson! I even asked the night clerk at the bus station just how my friend Henry Wilson was. He said, "Son, you must have been out of town. Everyone knows that Mr. Wilson is no longer with Drexel Furniture Company!"

I said, pointing to my two rows of ribbons on my uniform, "Yes sir, I have been out of town — for approximately two years!"

I was smashed beyond explaining. All my hopes and dreams had come to an abrupt end. Indeed, I would not be working for Mr. T. Henry Wilson. I took a taxi to my home on Avery Avenue and awakened my mother and dad saying, "I made it home, alive!" The next day my mother said, "I've got excellent news for you! You're going to Duke University!"

I said, "Mom, we don't have any money, and besides, I'm not qualified grade-wise."

She said, "Don't worry, you've had Latin and you've graduated from high school. We've applied for a G.I. free education for you."

I said, "But Mom, I don't think that my grades will get me in."

Mom replied, "We've been Methodists all of our lives, so I told our pastor (who was a Duke grad) that it is his responsibility to see that you are admitted." As it turned out, our pastor Fletcher Nelsons was a classmate at Duke with the man who had become registrar. His name was Charles Jordan, brother of later Senator Everett Jordan. He called Charlie and told him to look the other way when one Plato Wilson of Morganton came to be admitted to Duke. Fletcher said, "He's a good boy and he will graduate if given the chance." Mr. Jordan evidently did "look the other way," because I had no problem on entering Duke University in September 1946. I did graduate on time four years later. You just need some help along the way!

But before I entered Duke and right after my return from the war, my good and handsome friend Harold Mitchell, who had served in the European Theater with the U.S. Air Force, and I had an unbelievable time spending our "mustering out pay" on a marathon of double dating different girls each night. It required us to roam into three counties, but what fun we did have! At the end we were broke financially, and our eyes looked like four burnt holes in a blanket. You see, we had fallen way behind in our dating during the war years. Harold went on to Wake Forest College and then on to their law school. He has distinguished himself in that profession.

Now that my dreams of selling furniture for Henry Wilson had been dashed, I decided that I would be a civil engineer and build bridges over the Amazon River. Before entering Duke, I had obtained a job with the City of Morganton in the sewer department. I would learn something about levels and how sewer lines were laid out and executed.

One afternoon, after work, and waiting on my dear mother to cook supper, I lay down on the porch floor (in my dirty clothes and army brogans) to take a nap. I was awakened and looked up with surprise to see Henry Wilson! He said, "Pistol, you didn't come to see me when you arrived home from the army." I said, "Mr. Wilson, I was told that you were no longer employed." He replied, "We are located in an office down town and are starting a brand new factory named Hen-re-don (Henry, Ralph Edwards and Don Van Noppen). I want you to report to our construction foreman on Monday morning and help us pour cement footings for this new factory. I understand that you are going to Duke University. Consider studying these courses (he handed me a small piece of paper) and report to our factory superintendent each summer, while going to school, to learn the business." Another four-minute interview, to go with the first four minutes back in 1942, made a total of eight minutes with this extraordinary man whom I worshiped. I never saw Henry for the next four years, but I did exactly what he told me to do. Sheer blind faith!

When I next saw Henry Wilson was on the day I graduated from Duke. He was in the front row. He handed me the keys to a brand new Chrysler New Yorker and a most beautiful leather traveling bag. He said he wanted me to travel four states for Henredon Furniture Industries. Sometimes, if you dream big dreams and have some good help, they come true!

In September 1946, I entered Duke University. I could not begin to believe I was there and for free at that, due to the "G.I. Bill of Rights!" Even though the government paid us $65 per month to live on, I found out that there were other ways to enhance my monthly income. I set up a laundry pick-up and delivery business; a retail ice-cream sales business; a shoe repair agency and still had time to play sports and study.

I must tell you a little more about that ice cream business. Duke did not allow the students to be interrupted while studying. That meant no door-to-door salesmen. Duke's campus is located out in the Duke Forest, a long ways to go to pick up a snack to eat while studying, not to mention that very few students had autos. The market was there, in fact a captive one. So, I organized a sales staff of high profile athletes. I thought that no one would turn in or molest a star player. I bought the popsicles for 3 cents each, and we sold them for 10 cents each. One could make $50-$60 in about an hour! All went well until about one week before I was to graduate. A campus cop caught me unloading 144 gross of popsicles. He hauled me in to see the dean of men, Mr. Robert Cox. Well, before he could get the dean up and over to the university, it was approaching 11 p.m. I demanded that my popsicles be put into a freezer until the case was settled. They did so. Dean Cox, a very nice man, asked me why I had so many popsicles, and I replied that I was throwing a big party for all my friends. He was impressed that I had so many friends. He finally said that I should come into his office the next morning and we would discuss the matter. The upshot of the affair was that I convinced Dean Cox he should make it legal to sell treats to the students from 9 to 10 o'clock each night. He did so. I had dodged a bullet and was able to graduate on time. A little bit of salesmanship never hurts!

When I entered Duke University in 1946, I was sure that I could not join a fraternity, if asked, due to my limited funds. But, to my great surprise, my best friends during my freshman year were all asked to join the Kappa Alpha Fraternity, and I was included. By this time I had found many college jobs that enhanced my income, so I seized the opportunity to join the KA's. In retrospect, this was the best decision I made in college, in that my fraternity brothers became my best and life-time friends. As it turned out, they were the future leaders of our generation and remain today as real brothers. Being in the KA Fraternity afforded me much fun and many memories for a lifetime. What a group! We have gathered for the past 23 consecutive years to keep our friendships alive.

With my huge earnings in college, I was able to purchase a brand new Chevrolet in 1950. I might say, even with all the businesses I had, I finally made the Dean's List in my senior year. It surprised me, too. As earlier stated, Mr. T. Henry Wilson was at my graduation along with my family and girlfriend, Betty Cashion. A very happy milestone had been reached. I was climbing!

Now remember, I had only been around Mr. Wilson for eight minutes, two brief meetings, since I called on him in 1942 to sell him our yearbook advertisement, and he told me that he wanted me to sell furniture for him. Eight years had passed, but his promise was very much alive. The dream had come true. I believed in Henry Wilson, and evidently, he believed in me! Selling had become my game.

I started out as a temporary salesman for the former salesman, Joe Lee, who had been called back to the service as a captain and was sent to Korea. Joe was a fantastic golfer and didn't find too much time to work. I was able to double his sales in the year that he was gone. I was made the permanent salesman, and Joe was elevated to assistant sales manager of Heritage Furniture Company, High Point, NC. I found out that by "running scared" and working 12-15 hours a day I could succeed. I was having a 20-30 percent increase per year in my sales. I simply loved my job, and it was beginning to reward me financially. I always showed great respect for all my accounts and "serviced them to death." I put their welfare first and mine second. I soon learned that if you made the merchant money, he wanted to see you often

CHAPTER 2

Learning to Be a Professional Salesman

WHAT IS A SALESMAN? *By Paul Harvey*

A salesman is a pin on a map to a sales manager

A quota to a factory

An overloaded expense account to the auditor

A bookkeeping item called "cost of selling" to the treasurer

A smile and a wisecrack to the receptionist

And to buyers, a purveyor of the balm of flattery

A salesman needs the endurance of Hercules
> *the brass of a Barnum*
> *the craft of Machiavelli*
> *the tact of a diplomat*
> *the tongue of an orator*
> *the charm of a playboy*
> *and a brain as quick as UNIVAC*

He must be impervious to insult, indifference, anger, scorn, complaint and the effects of drinking all night with a customer.

He must be able to sell all day, entertain all evening and drive all night to the next town and be on the job fresh at 9 a.m.

He must be good enough to play and willing to lose at golf and cards and story-telling.

He wishes his merchandise were better. He wishes his prices were lower. He wishes his commissions were higher. His territory smaller. His competitors ethical. His goods shipped on time. His boss sympathetic. His advertising more effective. His customers more human.

But he is a realist and so realizes that none of this will ever be. But he is an optimist. So, he makes the sale anyway. He lives or dies by the daily report. He rolls his days away in a tedium of planes, trains and cars. He sleeps his nights away in a cheerless hotel room.

Yet, each morning he hoists onto his back the dead weight of last year's sales record, this year's quota, and goes forth to do it all over again. And yet, for all that, he can't for his life imagine anything he had rather do, anybody he'd rather be…than a salesman.

Chapter 2 – Learning to Be a Professional Salesman

*I*t had been nine years since I first had my dream of becoming a furniture representative for Mr. T. Henry Wilson at Drexel Furniture Company. Much had happened during these twisting and turning years: Graduating from high school; a war to fight in the South Pacific; dreams shattered by Mr. Wilson's leaving Drexel; a false start at becoming a civil engineer; a second meeting with Mr. Wilson; going to Duke University for four years and graduating in 1950; a full year of more training and getting married. Finally the day arrived in 1951 for me to begin my sales career with Heritage-Henredon Furniture Company.

I had just recently received the advice from Mr. Frank Wood, of the George T. Wood Carpet Company, a man in whom I had great confidence. He had advised, "Just be yourself if you want to be a successful salesman." On this first call as a professional salesman, somehow this advice didn't seem enough! I was very nervous because I so wanted to be successful. Many people were watching me and counting on me. I went out and purchased a sales manual and was in the process of reading it when one of my sales managers, Mr. Ralph Edwards of Henredon, told me he had selected Fowler Brothers Furniture of Chattanooga, TN for my first call. He had further told me that Mr. Calvin Fowler there was a proven and loyal customer and that I would not have any trouble with him.

With that, I headed for Chattanooga, reading my sales manual as I traveled. I finally was going to bat! Arriving in Chattanooga the next morning and being shown into Mr. Calvin Fowler's huge paneled office located in, what seemed to me, a half-a-block square store building that was five stories high, I found Mr. Fowler sitting at his enormous desk with his feet propped up on his desk. He did not look up from his morning newspaper. All around the paneled walls were very large framed pictures of prize-winning bulls. An idea flashed into my mind: I knew what my opening remarks would be. The sales manual said that you should talk on subjects of interest to your buyers. Well, I had milked four cows daily in my youth, so I would open with something that was of interest to us both!

I cleared my throat and said, " Mr. Fowler, I'm Plato Wilson, your new Heritage-Henredon salesman, and I see from the pictures on your wall that we both have an interest in cattle farming." With this remark, Mr. Fowler looked up and said, "Son, you didn't have to tell me that you were a farmer. You look like a hay seeder! "Now my knees began to shake and I realized that maybe my opening remarks had been poorly selected. So much for the sales manual. I somehow recovered to be "simply myself." Calvin told me to have a seat and tell him what I had on my mind. I launched into my rehearsed "pitch" about this brand new collection of furniture that I felt he would be interested in purchasing. He heard me out and said, "Son, I don't especially like what you have shown me; in fact it stinks, but you are so pathetic, if I do not give you an order, your company will let you go and I will not be able to train you to be fit to call on the retail trade!" He proceeded to give me a real good order, my first ever, of three to four pages in my order book. Then I remembered quotes from the sales manual, once again. I was handing him his copies of the order when I spoke out, "Mr. Fowler, my training tells me that a buyer should not buy on friendship, but rather on the merits of the product, and I feel you have done this for friendship reasons, and I do not feel right about taking this order."

With this Mr. Fowler tore the order into four pieces and tossed it into the waste can, my eyes following the pieces there. He said, "Son, you've learned your first lesson. Don't ever tell a buyer what he can or cannot buy. Just remember: Your name is Jimmy, you'll take what you Gimmie!"

Chapter 2 – Learning to Be a Professional Salesman

He then told me, "Son, drive back to Morganton, get out of your auto, get back into the auto and return to Chattanooga. Every time you pass over one of those expansion joints in the road, just repeat to yourself, "My name is Jimmy, I'll take what you Gimmie!" When you return here, I'll give you this same order that I have torn up."

I was a wreck. I'd blown my call and was far from being a professional salesman — if ever! I hastily drove back to Morganton, repeating the rhyme as I traveled. On arriving at the Henredon office, I went into Ralph Edwards's office to report "my version" of how the call had gone. I said to him, "Mr. Edwards, I think that I was able to get Mr. Fowler very excited over our new collection, and I really believe that on my next call I will obtain a nice order."

Ralph then blurted out, "I know all about your first call! Calvin Fowler has already telephoned me about what a 'hay seeder' you are, and that he tried to give you an order and that you advised him not to do so. Now get back into your auto and drive as fast as you can back to Chattanooga and get that order. We need it desperately." With this I was a double wreck! The world now knew what an amateur I was. My dream of being a professional salesman had dimmed quite a bit, but I still had grit, and now was the time to show it. Back to Chattanooga I went at double time. I secured the promised order and returned to the factory so that it could be promptly shipped. I had learned volumes in a short time, but evidently this was a hundred-volume series that I was to be exposed to before I even qualified just to be a salesman, let alone a professional one. But, I had made a beginning. One down and a million to go!

Not all of my furniture accounts were as large as Fowler Brothers. Many were small accounts that you had to be very careful in what you sold them and how much. You cannot sell very much to an account that is financially strapped. A salesman has to change gears and fully understand the account's ability to sell and pay for that which you are selling to them. The small dealer has to wear many hats: CEO, CFO, buyer, advertising executive, inventory controller, personnel director and sales manager. The salesman has to be familiar with all of these areas so as to help his client be successful. The salesman should be a good businessman and should be of immense help in all responsibilities of the client. You are an employee but not on the client's payroll. My ambition was to gain the full confidence of each client and never break that confidence. The client's welfare remained my number one goal for my entire career. If I was successful in making him money, he would take care of me as a by-product of our relationship. Dealers loved to see a salesman with this ability.

I soon learned, in my travels, that most retail salespeople were lacking in product knowledge and actually how to sell. I soon began to hold in-store sales meetings to teach these hungry sales people what they needed to know, not only to sell my product, but to sell all the products in their stores. I included motivational segments which gave them dreams of what they could become if they would apply their abilities learned. I could always motivate them for a month or so, but the real motivation that I told them was to have a personal goal that they wanted to accomplish such as sending their children to college, buying a better home or automobile, etc. This goal would motivate them when I was not there to kick start them!

These sales meetings were usually early in the mornings, before the stores opened. I would furnish coffee and donuts, at my expense, and all the fireworks. The attendance was usually 100 percent because they wanted to be better informed. I continued these sales meetings throughout my career since the store personnel was constantly changing. I took these meetings to a higher level when I invited them to our respective factories and called them "Sales Seminars." There they could tour factories and meet the key personnel and management of our companies. They even had the opportunity to have dinner with our presidents. I will discuss these seminars later in a special chapter entitled "The Seminars."

During my career, I bought many breakfasts, lunches and dinners for my clients. These events had at least a three-fold benefit: (1) they enriched our friendships, (2) we got to know the clients and their spouses better, and (3) they were a sort of a thank-you reward. I soon learned that time was very valuable and that the stores were only open eight hours a day. Time is the only thing that a salesman contributes to the product, so he should use it wisely. I arranged my territory into one-week "cloverleafs" (six leaves). This put me in touch with each account every six weeks, so they would not forget me. I printed postal cards — one for hotel reservations and the other for account appointments. I mailed them one week in advance of a trip. This worked well. I always arranged my calls each day to maximize the number of calls I could actually make. This sometimes required me to drive long distances at night so as to line them up for the shortest distance between accounts. Setting up my planning this way allowed me, as it relates to bowling, to knock down as many pins as possible in one day or with one ball! Some days, in more remote small towns, I could call on up to four accounts in one eight-hour day. That maximized my eight hours of open stores. Most of my days consisted of working anywhere from 12 to 18 hours. This consisted of an eight- hour workday in stores, entertaining for dinner, driving to the next city (sometimes 3-4 hours) and finally writing the orders and doing the paperwork. With a few hours of sleep, I awoke the next morning to do it all over again — just like Paul Harvey says in the opening of this chapter. I thrived on it and actually loved every moment of my career.

Before I began to actually start my traveling career, as I mentioned earlier, I went to my mentor and confidant, Mr. Frank Wood, who ran George T. Wood Carpet Distributorship in High Point and was a brother of the CEO of Heritage Furniture Company, for whom I was working. I asked Frank what I should do to be successful in selling. He simply said, "Be yourself, always!"

I said, "That's all?" He replied, "You have already come a long way just being yourself, so just continue. The public can spot a 'fake' so very easily." I tended to think this answer was simply too simplistic. As my career unfolded, it was indeed a marvelous piece of good advice. I have tried to follow this advice wherever my life took me.

Later, Elliot Wood, one of my bosses and the best salesman I ever knew, gave me some more excellent advice on how to become a better salesman every day. His solution was that on each and every call you make on a client, whether you get the order or not, you should get into your auto and pull off the road and analyze what happened. What phrase turned the sale into a sale? Or what phrase lost the order for you? Keep score of your winning phrases and your losing ones. Major in your "strong" points, and try to eliminate your "weak" points. I put this advice into action immediately and used it the rest of my sales career. It works! Some people go through life making the same mistakes over and over and never realize why.

One of the unusual experiences I had while working with Heritage-Henredon Furniture was in approximately 1953, when our company received the sole rights from the great world-class architect Frank Lloyd Wright to manufacture his designs for interior furniture. He allowed that all designs were derived from a circle, a square or a triangle. The collection of 50 or 60 designs was sent to us, reviewed by our designers, and then manufactured by us. They were not the most beautiful designs one would expect, but Heritage-Henredon thought the FLW name would carry the sales. The day came for the launching of the collection in off-season in our Chicago showroom. A FLW house was simulated in the showroom. Mr. Wright was to address the specially invited dealers from all over the nation at a luncheon in the Merchants and Manufacturers Club on the first floor of the

Chapter 2 – Learning to Be a Professional Salesman

Merchandise Mart. As he rose to speak, dressed in his usual cloak, part of the temporary platform collapsed. After the attendants quickly repaired the damage, Mr. Wright came to the podium and declared, "That's what I've been preaching all of my life – poor architecture!"

Prior to the luncheon, Mr. Wright had given us a "sales meeting" in our showroom. I happened to be sitting very close to the beautiful statue of Venus De Milo when Mr. Wright approached and said, "Now that is a true work of art." I instinctively said, "It sure is!" Without pausing, Mr. Wright turned to me and responded, "I thought you would say that." Even Mr. Wright appreciated a nude statue. This comment allowed even me to relate to and appreciate this famous architect.

One interesting thing about this special showing of the FLW collection was the fact that our event was hastily put together and our management was unaware that there were at least ten other nationwide trade shows going on in Chicago at that same time, and there were no hotel rooms to be had for love or money. Our company personnel and dealers had to make it a one-day event, with all travel plans to arrive early that morning and depart that same evening. What a mess in scheduling! On top of this, Ralph Edwards, our sales manager, had already written the dealers' orders before their arrival. Our salesmen just had to hand the orders out to our dealers, just what Ralph thought they needed. I had approximately 12 dealers that made it to the event. For the most part, everyone arrived and departed on their schedules. There was one exception; Mr. Oscar Seelbinder of Memphis, TN, presented me with a problem. He had a 9 p.m. train to catch back home. He had drunk too much. My flight departed at 7 p.m., so I had to leave Oscar at 6 p.m. I had an hour to walk him through the park near the train station in an effort to sober him up enough that he could get on the train by himself. After the walk, I sat him down on a park bench where he could easily see the tower clock at the nearby Union Station. I knew that he could not sit inside that hot station for three hours, and I also thought the cool air in the park would be good for him. I explained to Oscar that when the little hand rested on eight and the big hand on twelve, he should make his way to the station, with no luggage, and board the southbound train for Memphis. He allowed that he understood, and I took leave of him with great concern for having to leave him in his present condition. Next morning, back in High Point, NC, I called Oscar in Memphis and was delighted that he answered the phone and thanked me for my care. A salesman sometimes has to be a shepherd!

The FLW Collection didn't sell that well from the dealers' floors, and ultimately we marked the whole event off as a rather bad idea. Incidentally, the luncheon in Chicago was the only event in my long career that alcohol was ever served by my companies at a mid-day meal. This time, two drinks were served. Possibly Ralph Edwards thought the drinks would allow the "medicine" to go down easier. He could have saved the money that the two drinks cost since our listeners were in no mood for the medicine.

Handling complaints was one of the most difficult things I had to do early in my career. In the factories, quality was drilled into employees each and every day. When I hit the road to sell that quality product, I could not believe our factories made mistakes. The public is very demanding, especially when they pay high prices for a quality product. Still, we had complaints. I found, upon inspections in the homes, that some people just expect too much. I was having huge troubles settling these complaints. Then one day in Chattanooga, TN, someone explained to me how you settle complaints satisfactorily. He said clients get very upset with the smallest flaw in their furniture. If the complaint is not inspected quickly, they get even more upset. By the time you, the factory representative, finally reach them, it's a "federal case." He said the first thing to do is to appear and in a very low-keyed, nice way simply say, "Tell me all about this complaint." They blow off all of their steam, and then you say, "Is there anything else that you want to tell me?" In a few cases, they might be unreasonable, but in most cases, if the complaint is nominal, they simply say that you are so nice to come see the furniture and hear them out that, as their husband says, I don't think it's too bad and I think we can live with it. On the other hand, if the product is obviously bad, you just have it replaced. The friend further said, "Do in the beginning what you are going to do in the end and get credit for it." Listening is a great attribute.

Another very difficult thing a salesman has to deal with is changing distribution in a city. If your account is drying up and not putting forth the effort to sell your product which has been franchised to him, you must, sometimes, have to franchise another account in the trading area. Usually, hard feelings occur. I had to go all the way to China in 1977 to find how to do this without hard feelings. We were near the end of our three-week tour and were in Shanghai, staying in the apartments that Henry Kissinger and President Nixon had stayed and performed the Shanghai Accords between China and the U.S. The apartments were first class in every way and were furnished beautifully with antiques and works of art. We were to pack our bags and have them all in a first-floor apartment before breakfast, ready for departure. When we returned from breakfast, the Chinese man in charge of our tour said to all of us, "Some of you have overpacked your bags on departing your apartments. We will be in Shanghai all day. You might want to check your bags. You are free to do this in the course of the day. If the missing items do not show up, we cannot depart late this afternoon." Evidently the Chinese had each apartment inventoried and, while we were at breakfast, a check was made and the "overpacks" were reported. The Chinese are known for saving face of individuals. They knew exactly who had stolen the small art objects and could have put them on the spot, but this is not their way. Late that afternoon, we all gathered, not knowing whether we would be allowed to depart or not. As it turned out, the overpacks turned up and we departed on time. Not a word was said to anyone as to their overpacks.

Back to what I learned from this experience on changing franchises. I learned how to save face of the merchant that I was about to dismiss. I went to the merchant and told him that I had been a bad salesman to let his business deteriorate. I told him I thought he was a very good merchant but that I had let him down and it was my fault. The merchant said this was not true. He said it was his fault by taking too many other lines on and cutting my company's display. He said if I would give him a second chance, he would restore his past good business with me. Other times, the merchant would say that he had done a bad job for us and would understand if we removed our line from his store. Now, it was he who made the decision and not me. What a relief! In the first example, the dealer would fire himself up and do enormous business for me. I was the fall guy for a short while until the right solution was decided upon by the merchant. Those Chinese! I found out this solution works with friends, spouses, children or with other problems that arise.

My father taught me another great lesson in life about when you have an enormous problem that no solution seems to work. He took me to a big rock which was in our garden for years, and we had had to work around it and be frustrated. It was much too big to move, so we lived with it. He told me that the big rock was like big problems that I would have in my life. The solution for both was to take a sledge hammer and break either the rock or the problem into small particles that I could carry away or deal with. I used that theory for the rest of my life. Somewhere along the way, we encounter boulders, and now we know how to handle them.

Chapter 2 – Learning to Be a Professional Salesman

The "Rock Turning"

The story that I am about to relate began as an innocent childhood experience that grew to be a parable in the training of my retail sales forces many years later. In fact, it was probably my most quoted remark. It all began when I was about eight years of age and my father told me that he was going to take me fishing. This was a pleasant surprise in that my father seldom, if ever, joined me in activities for pleasure. Of course, there were strings attached. I was to secure every possible kind of bait: crickets, earthworms and spring lizards. I easily obtained the crickets and the earthworms and had them ready. The problem was locating the spring lizards. There was a branch located behind a neighbor's house (Sam Ervin II) that I thought would be productive for finding the lizards. I made my way to the location and, while intently looking, I did not see one spring lizard. Accidentally, I stepped on a small rock that was not secure and it flipped over, and much to my surprise, a couple of lizards scurried out from beneath it. Now I knew how to find more lizards! This completed the bait gathering. Dad and I had a great fishing trip at Lake James near Morganton. This turned out to be the one and only fishing trip we had together, so the memory had to last. Now back to the parable of selling. Racking my mind in ways to train our retail salespeople how to be go-getters and make good things happen, my mind finally went back to the spring lizards. I figured that the customers had to be searched for and if one were to be successful in finding them, one should "turn some rocks." Just waiting for one to appear was the wrong approach, so I thought I would tell this rock story in my sales meetings, hoping that the listeners would use the theory to take them to a higher level in sales. The lesson was to be proactive rather than reactive. Most of the listeners bought the idea and applied it in their efforts. I seldom visited a retail store, after telling this story, that someone wouldn't greet me with the remark, "I've been turning rocks!" Thanks to my dad, he had inadvertently taught me to be a better salesman, and in turn, I had intentionally passed it on to others.

However distracted my father's life was, he took the time to teach me how to work, and I was an eager student. He suggested jobs that I could do and helped me to schedule them even when I was at the tender age of nine and onward. I personally believe that this is the most valuable gift a father can give to his children. As a result of this gift, I was many years ahead of most of my generation. He taught me how to become street smart, either by his plan or our family's necessity. It was only later in my life that I attached the proper value to my father's gift to me at such a young age.

From the beginning of my traveling days, I decided that not many salesmen ever actually thanked, in writing, their accounts to show their appreciation for what they did for them. I began early to do something about this error in the industry. Since it was around January 20th before I received my yearly sales broken down in categories and at the same time, our presidents were making their "State of the Union" message to Congress, I decided that I would write a thank-you letter to all my accounts and include some advice on how I saw the coming year. I entitled the annual letter "THE STATE OF THE TERRITORY."

In these letters, I first thanked the dealer and his staff for making my year excellent and also that of my factories. I broke their sales down in the various categories and showed a three-year comparison, so the dealer would know in which direction his sales were going. If the figures were advancing, the dealers were happy and wanted to buy even more of our product. If his figures were receding, he and I needed to talk about how to improve them. Actually, most of the accounts did not have any idea how much business they did with me until they received these letters. In jest, the dealers kidded me that these letters were their "report cards" from me. I wrote some 45 of these annual letters in my career. I am including several of these letters in the appendix in the back of this book.

In the first 10 to 15 years of my sales career, I would send all of my accounts some small remembrance at Christmas time. Then, more and more would ask me why I didn't send them much larger gifts at Christmas. When this happened, I decided to stop the gifts all together. I did not choose to be in the "payola" business.

Our family used our little mountain cottage, Timbuktu as an entertaining retreat for our accounts and their staffs, including spouses and children. These events were usually held on Wednesday afternoons (when stores closed back then) or on Sundays. All dealers within easy driving distance (50-60 miles) would come, and I would cook steaks, grill pork chops and add country ham and fried chicken. These events were a big hit with everyone, especially family members. I think that the largest of these affairs was 50 people from Mecklenburg Furniture Shops in Charlotte, NC. Most were around 15 to 20 persons. My dear wife and I did most of the work. It was quite a chore to ask a spouse to do. But, our family profited with better homes, autos and living standards, not to mention college educations for two children in private universities.

I slowly was getting better on my way to becoming a professional salesman. Sales were growing by an average of 10-12 percent per year. I began to keep a posted graph of my personal sales, year by year. As the line ascended, this was my real compensation and joy. My driving goal was, in the end, to have people say, "He was a professional." Your reputation is all that you end up with, after all is said and done. A good reputation consists of your faith, your honesty, your family relations, your character and, of course, your overall success. An excellent reputation is worth the price you are willing to pay for it.

My greatest fear, always, was that I might fail. By running scared, I always worked harder. As I grew in success, I could not handle hearing anyone say, "He used to be good." I learned that you have to keep on doing better. One never stands still. Like rowing a boat upstream, you're either going up or you're going back. Upon graduating from high school, our class motto was "The higher you climb, the broader the view." I accepted that then and continued to believe it for the rest of my career.

Selling is a lot like sports. A player can score three touchdowns on a given Saturday, and the stands applaud. On the next Saturday when the player fails to score any touchdowns, those same fans are apt to boo him. How fickle life is, but it's that way. I adopted a truism that I told myself every morning: "You're as good as your last day's performance." That will motivate you and keep you from resting on your laurels. This slogan is true in all aspects of life: being a Christian, a better spouse, parent and friend, or anything else you attempt to do.

In the development of becoming a professional salesman, I learned a great many lessons:

From my good friend, Clyde Powell of Columbia, SC, I learned vital, common sense lessons. Clyde was a very plain man with uncommon wisdom. He was not a direct account of mine, but he had financial interest in a couple of regular franchised accounts that I called on. When I was in need of some down-home logic on sensitive problems, I always managed to visit Clyde to obtain his simple solutions. Here, for instance, are a couple:

(1) Clyde had a controlling interest in one of my accounts in Charleston, SC, with the minority interest held by the manager. I asked Clyde how he handled the compensation of this manager. His answer was that he paid the manager a good living salary and then gave him a 25 percent annual bonus of the net profit, but only if the business had the cash to pay the bonus. This stipulation would control overbuying.

(2) He required his manager to write the cost of each item sold,

daily, on the back of the sold ticket to be subtracted from the selling price. That would be the gross profit. From the gross profit a flat 25 percent (yearly overhead) was subtracted to obtain the net profit. At the end of the day, the manager and Clyde both would know how much profit the store made each day. Clyde called this "closing the books each day." Most merchants had to wait until the end of the month, or in some cases, the end of the year, before they realized their financial condition. Both of these vital solutions worked beautifully and resulted in superb management, with more motivation assured. I was able to pass these solutions on to other small merchants. It is always good to know people of wisdom.

Another big problem that I discovered in my career was that of a family business with many children. The founding father, at his death, would leave the business to all of his children. Some of the children chose other professions, and some just were not qualified to add to the future of the company. At the same time, they all shared equally in profits despite the fact that only one or two actually worked in the business. This brought on hard feelings for the ones who had the responsibility of producing the profits and having to share with those who did not work there. The problem was squarely on the father who should have avoided this bad situation by dividing his estate in a more equitable fashion.

I was able to advise many of the founders of a way around this bad situation. I suggested that they ask each child at a family gathering, if they were interested in coming to the business each and every day to insure the store's success. Out of five children, possibly one or two would answer the call to be real merchants. The others were compensated with other financial assets for their share of their mothers' and fathers' estates. In this solution, only the real believers took over the business and usually ran very successful operations and were rewarded fairly for their efforts. The other family children took their assets and worked at other endeavors. As a result, all family members were happy, and the family remained respectful of each other.

I was able to help many families to accomplish this plan. In some cases, however, it would take two or three years of my persistence to persuade the father to actually divide the estate fairly. People simply put off drawing up a will that requires thought. They do not want to think about death or to face hard facts.

The fathers and mothers who did execute my plan were very proud of themselves for having done so. You cannot believe how many telephone calls and letters I received from happy children thanking me for my persistence. I considered it was my duty as I had seen too much pain from families in my early career. Sometimes one just has to meddle in other people's lives when they love and respect them. It helps, however, to be on good terms with them. I never lost any friends by going out on this limb. I can remember one dear friend that I failed to convince.

Thomas Haxley: *"The rung of a ladder was never meant to rest upon, but only to hold a man's foot long enough to enable him to put the other foot somewhat higher."*

From General Eisenhower, I learned: *"In any endeavor, one should plan and prepare until the last hour, lest he lose it all."*

From Henry Wadsworth Longfellow: *"Not in the clamor of the crowded street, not in the shouts and plaudits of the throng, but in ourselves are triumph and defeat."*

From a former neighbor, Senator Sam Ervin II, as told to him by Robert Patton, his one- room schoolmaster: *"The world is a grindstone — whether you let it grind you down or polish you up, depends on you."*

From T. Henry Wilson Sr.: *"If you have two weeks in which you have to make a final decision, wait until the final hour to announce it."* He elaborated on this: *Situations and events can change that could change your decision. Of course it would be proper to study your decision and make it earlier, but just don't announce it until the last hour."*

Salesmanship: *"The transfer of a conviction to a willing party."* The "willing party" is a result of the salesman's having cultivated and conditioned the "party" to become a "willing party."

The Essence of Salesmanship: People have asked me why was I able to make so many sales? There are no silver bullets. It is very hard to put into words their essence. But one on one, a salesman and a buyer, there is a method that seldom failed me: The salesman has to get into the head of the buyer and find out where he is, what is his present condition and what is his mood. One obtains these answers by asking many subtle questions slowly. When these answers are obtained, the salesman then makes the proper pitch. You fill his needs by entering his own mind. Think about this! If you wanted to go to Atlanta, you would not get into your car and head out to Nashville, TN. You would consult a map and drive the most direct route to Atlanta. Many sales are lost when a salesman just confronts the buyer and gives him a canned pitch that doesn't fit the buyer. One size doesn't fit everyone!

In selling anything, one should sell the concept and the uniqueness of the product. This sometimes is called "the sizzle." Selling individual components or individual items will never get one the big payoff, because the average salesman does it this way. In selling the total concept, the buyer can shape a vision of the product for himself and for you, the seller. The value is established as long as you, the salesman, insure continued value through high quality service and stimulation. The fire will continue as long as the salesman feeds the fuel.

CHAPTER 3

My Friend
T. Henry Wilson Sr.

A Dream to Sell

I first heard of Henry Wilson, no relation of mine unfortunately, in about 1934 when he came to Morganton, NC, to be president of Drexel Furniture Company in Drexel, NC. Drexel was almost broke. It was owned mostly by the Huffman and Kistler families. One of the first things Henry did was to start manufacturing 18th century furniture (Travis Court) and storing it in every warehouse available to him. One could not believe how many were available due to the many bankruptcies there were, as a result of the 1929 crash. He bet all of his chips on the theory that when the economy finally was restored that 18th century furniture, the staple of the furniture industry, would sell if anything would sell. Furniture employees were lucky if they made anywhere between 40 and 60 cents an hour. So, his cost was very low and he could afford to warehouse the finished products. His bet also assumed that when the economy did pick up, his competitors would have much higher costs than he had had and that he could "eat their lunches." People around Morganton thought Henry Wilson had lost his mind.

He had rented an old house on West Union Street and had moved his wife, Dell, and the children into this house. The economy did pick up by the mid- and late-thirties. Henry was ready. His bet had paid off and now the people of the town came around to the belief that Henry was really smart after all! In approximately 1939, a North Carolina newspaper announced that Henry Wilson, president of Drexel Furniture Company was the highest paid executive in the state — $125,000.00 per year. Henry was totally embarrassed.

I was told that Henry Wilson, when he first made big money, paid off his father's debt at the bank in Gastonia, NC. This debt had long been written off by the bank, but Henry wanted to clear his father's name. This was, indeed, the measure of the man, Henry Wilson Sr. One does not find many in life with his character.

My first business dealing with Henry Wilson was not a face-to-face one. I was about 13 years old. Henry, by this time in 1937, had built a new home on Powe Street in Morganton and needed some cow manure for his rose garden. Somehow he heard I had such a business and called me and ordered a wagonload. At the time I gave him the price of $2.50. I delivered the manure and waited for my check. Much time elapsed and still no check. I called him to tell him he was past due on his account. He then explained that he had not received an invoice for the manure. I told him that I thought the manure pile, at his back door, was proof enough that I had delivered. He then said for me to send him a bill and he would pay me. I took a page out of my "Blue Horse" notebook and sent him the bill marked Past Due. He paid me promptly. I still had not met the man face-to-face. I was learning about businesses and collection departments.

My very first face-to-face meeting with Henry Wilson was the story that I related in Chapter 1. This meeting, in his office at Drexel Furniture Company had a four-minute duration that ultimately put me in a career that filled me with joy — selling furniture for the renowned T. Henry Wilson Sr.

Henry Wilson was a native of Gastonia, NC, where his father ran a large livery stable from which people rented horses and buggies. This was a large business since it provided the main mode of travel. His father expanded the business into a mail delivery service into the neighboring states and regions. As a small boy, Henry would go with the mail drivers to make deliveries. He related to me that he was taught by some of these black drivers that when camping out, en route, one should go to bed, on the ground, with his head instead of his feet to the fire. The head has the most heat loss. As a result of this training, Henry, when he traveled with me, would often put a wool toboggan on his head when he slept. A practical lesson learned should be remembered.

Henry graduated from Davidson College in approximately 1929 — with honors. In the '29 crash, Henry's father almost lost his last dollar, mostly because he had co-signed notes at the bank for so many of his many friends. The bank called for his payments. As a result, his father was so depressed that he met an early death.

In spite of this, Henry, somehow, was able to attend Harvard University in Boston by working his way through this distinguished university. In the summers, he obtained a union card and worked on cruise ships between New York City and England. His specialty was as a salad maker. He graduated from Harvard with an MBA — with honors, once again!

Back in Gastonia, he went to work for the same bank where he had later repaid his father's bad debts. His job, in this greatly depressed time, was to travel in Western North Carolina to call on businesses that needed loans. A lot of these businesses were furniture manufacturers. In the process, he met and fell in love with Dell Bernhardt of Lenoir. He later married her and went to work for her father at Bernhardt Furniture Company.

He improved the conditions at Bernhardt greatly until jealousy developed with his brothers-in-law. He then went down the road to Drexel Furniture where he obtained the job of sales manager. Success followed. In fairly short order, however, Henry was called back to Bernhardt a second time. Progress was being made with Henry's return. Jealousy reoccurred, and he was fired once again. He went back to Drexel Furniture still again, this time as president. His success there was enormous.

During WWII, to keep the Drexel Furniture Company busy and also to obtain materials, he devoted some space to making plywood gliders for the war effort. This helped save the company from disaster.

During WWII, Henry and his key associates tried to buy out the stockholders of Drexel. This was unsuccessful, and their positions were either terminated or abandoned. Henry and his staff decided to open up their own factory. At Drexel Furniture Company on Christmas cards and letters, Henry, Ralph Edwards and Don Van Noppen had signed these documents as: Henry Ralph and Don. They were well known and respected in the national industry, so they decided to name the new company "Henredon." Sterling Collett, a Harvard graduate as well, was still in service of his country, but chose not to have his name included in the new furniture company. Of course, he planned to be a part of the new venture. Materials were hard to come by to build the new factory as were supplies to operate it. All concerned had such great faith in these men starting the venture that they pledged their efforts to make it happen.

Henry hit the road to sell both preferred stock and common stock to any friend who would listen. He worked in Gastonia, NC, and High Point, NC, very hard. Many friends in Gastonia believed in Henry Wilson, among them the Ragan family. All became very rich as the new company was very successful.

Henry Wilson was, indeed, a man with many excellent talents — one of the most important as a personnel manager. He contracted for all key personnel for the factory and most all other jobs. Henredon was blessed by his choices in every area.

When I went to work for him, he told me, "I have sought you out for your abilities and I think you will succeed. I am a very busy man and will not be able to supervise you. However, I have confidence in you. If you ever get in trouble in your job, come to me and I will help you solve your problems."

Well, I thought this was my personal speech. I later found out that he told every new employee the same story. He was a quiet leader and motivator. None of us felt we ever needed help due to his confidence placed in our selection, a great practice which most employers should follow. I was beginning to learn that Henry Wilson was the man whose rising star I was so happy to be hitching my sled to. One can only be as good as the honest leader he works for. "How can you soar with eagles when you work with turkeys?" Henry Wilson was, indeed, an eagle, and I hoped to soar with him.

Throughout my friendship with Henry Wilson, he never let me down. He quietly opened doors for me without my knowing it. Even today, when I see an automatic opening door, I think of Henry and marvel at his help in the past. Henry also taught me how to invest my earnings. He took the time to make a trip to New York City with wife Betty and me to meet a fabulous investor at Marine Midland Grace Bank, Mr. Charles Robbins, who had advised Mr. Grace of the famed Grace Cruise Lines, to invest his millions wisely. Henry had entrusted millions with Mr. Robbins. On our original meeting Henry simply said to Mr. Robbins, "This little fellow and his wife have a shirttail full of dollars. Help them multiply these assets and treat them as my children." He returned to North Carolina and left us to establish our future with Mr. Robbins. This was Henry's last of many gifts to me, for he died shortly afterward with heart failure. He was still a very young man — approximately 67 years old. What a man and what a friend!

I value the memory of yet another event that demonstrated the wisdom of Henry Wilson. It was a cold December afternoon in 1967 around 5 o'clock that I happened to be at the Henredon factory and was asked by Henry to accompany him on one of his frequent walks around the mile-long road that circled the factory. The wind was blowing as we walked, and I asked Henry if he ever thought the factory would be this large when he built the first phase in 1946. I received no reply. Knowing that Henry had diminished hearing in one ear (I never could remember which one) from an early life automobile accident, I crossed over to his other side and asked the same question. Still, I received no answer. I let it drop, and we continued our walk, talking about other subjects. Finally, on the backside of the factory, Henry walked towards the boiler room. In the manufacturing of "casegoods" (wood furniture), the boiler room is the heart and soul of the facility in that it burns the lumber waste and sawdust, heats the plant and makes the steam that runs the various clamps and drying rooms. Henry walked into the boiler room, and I followed. He asked me how many boilers we had in this room when we opened it back in 1946. I answered that we had one. He asked me to count the present boilers in operation. I counted six. Nothing else was said, and we departed the boiler room. I soon realized that Henry had just given me his answer as to the expected future size of the factory. Back in 1946, he started with only one boiler but built the boiler room large enough to accommodate six. That is wisdom and vision! Many of Henry's answers to my questions over the years came in the same fashion. Henry Wilson's idol and mentor was Alfred Sloan, the man who combined many trademark auto companies into one to form General Motors. Henry once told me that one of the many lessons learned from the study of Alfred Sloan came from Sloan's story about the biggest mistake in his mid-career. This was the matter of not building facilities large enough and expandable in the original planning. Henry did not make this mistake, as is evident in the boiler room story nor in other facilities he erected in his lifetime. Uncommon wisdom and vision this friend of mine, Henry Wilson, had.

Much to my surprise, while traveling in Charleston, SC, I received a very early morning telephone call at the Hotel Sumter; I was advised that Henry Wilson had died and left instructions for me to be one of his pallbearers. I was shocked, surprised and elated, in that Henry could have any important businessman in the U.S. to be his pallbearer, but he chose me for one. Henry had been a member for years of the board of the Federal Reserve Bank in Richmond, VA, associating with the best in finance. Why me? As it turned out, Henry had requested, as pallbearers, one person from each major department of Henredon to carry his final remains. What a final show of expression to the company employees who helped him succeed!

Flashbacks at the man I loved.

In traveling with Henry in Tennessee (he loved to go out there and travel with me, especially to see his long time buddy, Mr. Lip Davis of Davis Cabinet Company), I asked Henry why he chose to call me his friend when I was neither on his brain level or his financial level. He simply said, "You tell it like it is, always. I have too many people around me that are 'yes men.' I know what I know, I really want to know what others think." My mind flashed back to my first meeting with him when I told him that he was making the mistake of his lifetime when he didn't want to purchase that first ad in our first yearbook at Morganton High School, and he was president of Drexel Furniture Company.

Another flashback that I had, at the time of his death was when I asked Henry, "What is a genius? I've heard many people say you are a genius." He simply said that he didn't know what a genius was. About 100 miles down the road as we traveled, out of the blue, he said, "I can give you the definition of a dumb man and a smart man." He said a dumb man, even well-educated, would answer a very simple question with a very complex answer to show every one how smart he was. No one understood the answer. On the other hand, a smart man being asked a very complex question would render a very, to-the-point, simple answer that everyone understood. Now we know why he was so successful. He was, indeed, a very smart man approaching a genius. That was my friend T. Henry Wilson Sr.

My final flashback: As we attended Henry's funeral in the chapel of the First Presbyterian Church, Morganton, the chapel was a story in itself. Henry and Dell Wilson had wanted to make a sizeable contribution to the building of the new church complex. The original plans called for a church building, Sunday school and a chapel. The Wilsons thought, with their sizable contribution to the building campaign, that maybe others in the church might tend to hold back on their giving and maybe the chapel would not get built. So the Wilsons corrected this by earmarking their gift to build the chapel only. Thus the membership had to dig deep to secure the necessary funds to build the church building and Sunday school. It all was completed as Henry and Dell wished, originally. Quite a well thought-out plan. Henry's mind was still working.

CHAPTER 4

Tricks of the Trade

A Dream to Sell

Throughout my 44 years in the furniture industry as a manufacturer's representative, I learned many "Tricks of the Trade." In retrospect, they all seem practical and common-sense solutions that helped me be a more professional salesman. The real trick was to make them a part of your everyday life. They all worked for me. I am listing below some of these tricks. They are listed randomly and not in any particular order:

1. *"Your customers will pay for your fashion clothes,"* said my Uncle Harry. I thought he was just giving me a sales pitch since he was in the clothing business. As it turned out, he gave me good advice in that customers liked well-dressed salespeople.

2. To sell fashion, you have to dress fashionably. This is closely related to No. 1 above. Most of my career, I sold upholstery (sofas and chairs) that fell into the high fashion category. These buyers are very fashion-conscious. They were not in the mood to buy from a poorly dressed salesperson.

3. Packing your traveling bag for a trip is most important. I wore a fresh shirt every day. I took three freshly pressed suits for a week. I had a bath each morning, shined my shoes, had a haircut often, cleaned my nails and wore a smile on my face. You would be surprised how many salesmen do not do this.

4. Dress appropriately. When I was just out of college I traveled in conservative suits, knowing that my buyers were much older than I. As I grew older, I dressed in sportier clothes in an effort to look younger.

5. Promptness. Being late can cause you to lose your appointment. Client's time is valuable, and he has allotted you just a short time to make a call.

6. Maximize your number of calls a day. The more calls you make in a day, the more business you obtain. There is the old "Beechnut Chewing Gum" theory: If you make ten calls a day, you will at least receive eight orders.

7. Always look up to the buyer. They are very, very important! To constantly remind me of this, I bought one of those little fuzzy animal heads that have the eyes that roll around and attached it to the lid of my sample case. The eyes always looked up when I opened the case.

8. Know your line and always be prepared. I learned this in Boy Scouts. It also works in selling.

9. Think positively. Your positiveness is contagious. One has to "uplift" the buyer.

10. Honesty – always. My mother taught me early on: "Son, always tell the truth because you are not smart enough to tell lies."

11. The essence of selling: The transfer of a conviction to a willing person.

12. Find your customer on the buying scale. Some accounts are small but they buy big. Others are large but buy small. One has to know the tolerance of the buyer and fit the sales pitch to that tolerance.

13. Adjust to the size of the account. One of the most difficult things for a salesman to do is "change gears" in his presentation. If one has just left a huge account and is about to call on a much smaller one, it is necessary to "gear down," otherwise your "high" will discourage the smaller account.

14. Be a partner to your accounts. Make the account money at no expense to him. Bring the account new and fresh ideas. Help the buyer be successful.

15. Train his sales staff. Arrange interesting and knowledgeable sales meetings and seminars. You are helping him do his work.

16. Be unique. Just being another pretty face in the crowd will not get you too far in the selling business. You have to be a unique, one-of-a-kind individual that separates you from the crowd. One's style and flair has to be recognized.

17. Deliver good newspaper advertisements, from distant areas, that were successful. The account needs stimulation. Ideas are stimulating as well.

18. Be persistent. Shy salespersons never succeed. I developed the "Six Door Approach":
    1. Try the front door,
    2. The back door,
    3. The side door,
    4. The basement door,
    5. A window and finally,
    6. The coal chute door. Finally, the buyer will understand that you really have something to say and will let you in.

19. Be imaginative. On each trip bring new ideas and some clean new jokes to make the account smile.

20. Know that selling is hard work. It really requires 12-15 hours per day. Example: I had a big buyer in Knoxville, TN named Bill Bell who preferred to work with me after the store closed at 5 p.m. We worked for a couple of hours, and then he wanted me to take him to dinner. This brought us to 9:30 p.m. and I still had four hours to travel to Nashville before I did the paperwork and went to bed. That was at 2:30 a.m. This schedule was not unusual when traveling a large territory. The orders keep you going!

21. Selling casegoods is much easier than selling upholstery. First of all, the origin of the term "casegoods" comes from the funeral business. In off-seasons, the funeral case builders would make chests and dressers or casegoods. That is why in the early days of the furniture business you found a funeral home and next to it was their furniture store. A few of the combinations still exist today. One has to sell the sofa or the chair at least three times for one order: Select the frame style; select the fabric; and finally select the cushion type and trim. At any point, it is possible to lose the sale. If the buyer likes the design and wood on casegoods, you are able to sell 20 or 30 correlated pieces just like shooting fish in a barrel! Usually factories pay higher commissions for selling upholstery.

22. Lay out your suggested upholstery order before you see the buyer. Lay out best-selling upholstery frame pictures on the floor. Put the proper sofa and chair together and then select the suggested fabrics for the correlation. If one is pretty good at doing this, he is assured of a good order and in a much shorter time frame. You are helping the buyer to do his job. I learned that the buyers would tire and would stop buying at about half of what he needed to buy. It is the best and most productive way to sell upholstery furniture.

23. Enlighten sales staff in your account while you are waiting to see the buyer. Most of the time your buyer is delayed in seeing you at the appointment time. Then, sometimes, they just make you wait. I spoke with the floor salesmen about the product and what was new. I also updated the store's catalogs and fabric samples. I made sure the store had current price lists and production schedules. I used, effectively, all of my time that I was in the account. Time is money!

24. Spend time with warehousemen and delivery staff. They can make a road salesman and his factory look good or bad. They

can touch-up a little scratch or bruise on your product without anybody's knowing about it. They also display the product on the showroom floor. They can select a good spot or a
bad spot. Make real friendships with these wonderful people.
Most road men do not!

25. Take time to go over your company's advertisement schedule
with your buyer. He may want to buy the pieces in the ad for
his floor display. Example: Mr. Larry Hendricks would buy
one-half dozen ad collections, put one collection on his floor
and "nail it down." He then delivered duplicates from his
warehouse. This method of buying not only speeds up the
delivery process, but makes his customers very happy.

26. Never write an order in the store. The way you handle this
is to record the order in a notebook and later, at your leisure,
record it officially on the formal order books. This saves the
salesman much time and allows him to make more calls.
Another liability of writing in the store is that it might look,
to the dealer, that he has bought too much as he sees you on
the fourth or fifth page of your order book! Let me stress
that honesty must be the rule of this practice. Never, ever,
pad an order!

27. You can't chase women and drink a lot of whisky! Both of
these activities are full time jobs! Furthermore, they lead to
immorality. A salesman sometimes has too much time on his
hands at night. Temptation abounds. I choose to travel every
night to eliminate the problem. "An idle brain is the devil's
workshop."

28. Display and square footage in the account is the very key.
Fight constantly for more and better space.

29. Do favors for the floor salespersons and become their friends.
They sell the product of their favorite sales representatives.
Besides, it's nice to have friends!

30. Know your retail salespersons by their names. At one time in my career, I had over 600 retail salespersons to remember. To make this more difficult, they moved from store to store. I developed a system that made it possible for me to know them and keep up with them in their moves: I kept a little black book. For every account I listed the salesperson's name and some identification trait (glasses, thin, short, etc.). Just before I went into the account, I checked my black book. I took this a step further. I studied all the acknowledgments and invoices of the account to be called on to see what salesperson had on special order for his or her customers. Example: Mabel Smith/ Dr. and Mrs. John Brown would be on the order. I would go up to Mabel and thank her for the beautiful dining room suite that she sold to the Browns. My retail salespeople could not believe that I was that smart to remember this. They didn't know that I had a "system."

31. Check the store's warehouse for sold goods awaiting delivery. This was the first thing that I did on arriving at the account. I would make a list of sold items, items missing from the floor space and also things that I wanted especially to sell him. I had a pretty good order, already, before I started with the buyer. This helped the buyer as well.

32. Remember: *"Selling is a high calling!"* To be able to communicate effectively is what life is all about. All successful professional salespeople, doctors, lawyers, engineers, scientists, and preachers have to be great communicators. Selling is a most honorable profession if it is done correctly.

33. My motivation, originally, was to make money. After I did this to some degree, I decided that being a reputable professional salesman was much more my motivation. Regardless of your money, your reputation is all that counts. A good honest reputation should be one's highest priority.

34. A salesman's time is all that he adds to the product. One should use this time very wisely. The salesman is highly paid for his time and results.

35. Always remember, *"You're only as good as your last day's performance."*

36. If it is going to happen, it's up to the salesman to make it happen. The factory back home is awaiting your results.

37. Develop good wholesome habits and keep them for your lifetime. They never go out of style!

38. Never knock a competitor or his product. Always treat them with kind words and deeds. They can, likewise, help you.

39. I think that selling is very similar to sports. One gets knocked down and has to get up fast and go again. One cannot dwell on bad calls by the referee, just keep playing the game. The final results will be recorded on the scoreboard!

40. Remember: *"A friend is a present you give yourself!"* Make and keep many.

41. When you are in a race, or a business, never trip your competitor. If you do, and you win the race, you really will not know if you were the best. Play the game honestly!

42. ALWAYS BE YOURSELF!

43. DARE TO BE EXCELLENT!

CHAPTER 5

My Friend Calvin Fowler

A Dream to Sell

I introduced to you earlier my friend Calvin Fowler of Chattanooga, TN, from that first call I made on him. It was always a circus! He was a very wealthy man and had married a wonderful lady from Nashville. They made a very understanding couple.

Calvin's father and his Uncle Frank of Knoxville founded Fowler Brothers Furniture Company (separate corporations). Later, brother Jimmy in Nashville also went into the furniture business, but not nearly in the scope of Fowler Brothers. His firm was named "Period Furniture Company." Both Fowler Brothers stores dominated the furniture business in Tennessee, especially the one in Chattanooga. If a company's representative was going to be successful, he had to be in their stores.

Calvin's store in Chattanooga was five stories tall. The warehouse, on the main railway in another location in the city, was the largest known in the industry. I was told that 23 boxcars could be unloaded at one time. They were wholesalers of appliances and furniture to the Mid-South. They were big and important.

One Christmas, my wife gave me a brand new pair of cordovan horsehide shoes that were very expensive. I wore them on my next call on Calvin. Naturally I was all shoes. Calvin spotted the new shoes, and an idea developed in his practical trick mind. He said to me, "Son, I want you to take a trip with me!" We got into his Olds and started out of town. He stopped at a feed store, and we went in. He purchased a huge sack of shelled corn (100 lbs.), and I put it in his trunk. We were headed for his big farm named River Bend. At the entrance there were barns, sheds and huge pastures with many cattle grazing. He stopped and told me to get out and do him a huge favor. It seems that a spring drain had stopped up and the area was very marshy. He instructed me to get a shovel out of the barn and clean out that spring drain. Now, remember, I was dressed fit to kill and wearing those fine new shoes. *A salesman has to do what he has to do in order to sell his important store*, I thought to myself. So I went at it as Calvin roared off to the farmhouse with the shelled corn in the trunk. Early on I could see that my shoes were going to be trashed in all that mud and water. I finally finished and looked a mess! I walked up to the farmhouse. On seeing me, Calvin looked at my new shoes and said, "Son, you've ruined your shoes, it looks like!" I quickly told him that they would clean up and for him not to worry. He then said, "Don't worry, son, I'm going to give you an order that will allow you to buy 50 pairs of new shoes!" Well, the day was not over yet. We went out to his Olds, and he told me to shoulder that 100 pounds of shelled corn and that we were going up-land to his man-made lake to feed the ducks. I did, and we went to the lake, which was quite a distance. Back to the city and store — he was as good as his word, and I received probably a $150,000 order. Sometimes you have to give your all to be successful and stay in with your big accounts!

On another visit with Calvin, there was a little recession in progress, and times were tough. Henredon had a brand new collection named "Cherry Casual," and I needed to place this line with Fowlers. It was a very sellable collection. The store had long benches and chairs outside Calvin's huge office. Early each morning, each traveling sales-man tried to be the first in the store and secure the seat nearest to Calvin's office door. Well, I was about third in line when Calvin arrived. He promptly announced that he was not buying anything today, because he was overbought. The benches and chairs emptied and left me sitting there. I had to see Calvin! At noon Calvin came out of his office on his way to lunch and saw me still sitting there. He said, "Son, didn't you hear me this morning when I said that I was not buying anything?" I said that I had, but that I had something important to talk with him about. He instructed me to leave. Well I did and went to lunch by myself. I resumed my seat outside his office for all the afternoon. Calvin did not return from lunch. The next day I took my seat outside his office with at least 10 more new salesmen. Again, Calvin arrived and made the same announcement that he made yesterday — no buying! The seats cleared except for me. I sat there all day and was not asked in. The third day I was back again. Calvin came in and dismissed all the salesmen and called me into his office. He said, "You are the dumbest salesman I've ever seen. I told you three times that we were not buying and you continue to stay. What's wrong with you?" I said, "Mr. Fowler, I have something so important to talk with you about that you just have to hear it." He said, "Nothing is that important!" I said maybe my presentation of my new hot collection is! I opened my bag and presented the collection. He ended up buying $75,000 worth of it and put me on my way. On leaving he said to me, "Son, you might make a salesman out of yourself yet." Perseverance had paid off!

One Christmas I sent Calvin one of my father's celebrated country hams. He loved it! The next fall on one of my six-week calls, he said he would like to buy some of my father's hams to give away. I was flattered for my father. Calvin yelled out to his secretary to type up the purchase order. Somehow, she typed in 100 hams. She knew what a big buyer he was. I thought no more about the order and gave it to my father to ship. All was well, I thought. Right after Christmas I went to the Chicago Furniture Market. Calvin stayed at the Palmer House as did all the Henredon people. I was given a note on checking in at the hotel that I was to call Calvin Fowler in room 1011. I could not imagine for what. When I got him on the phone he said, "What do you want to do with the extra country hams that I have in my room up here? I only ordered 10 and you shipped 100!" I was scared to death. I said, "Calvin, I just delivered your purchase order to my father and he filled it." He said, "Someone put an extra zero on the order and I received 100!" I really thought he had the hams in his room, so I went up to his room to straighten the matter out. On entering the room I did not see any country hams, but Calvin was sitting in a lounge chair laughing. He said, "Son, I fully enjoyed giving those 100 hams away for Christmas, and my friends certainly did enjoy them!" Once again he had played a practical joke on me and had me on the brink. That was my friend Calvin Fowler at his best. For my worries over "the country ham scam" he gave me a supermarket order before he left town.

Calvin's jokes were not just for me. His assistant manager was a North Carolinian from Asheville named Richard Worley, who had married into the Fowler family. "Fish" (his nickname) was a very careful and detailed person — all business. He loved baseball and dreamed of seeing a big league World Series. Calvin knew this and came up with the idea that Richard should go to New York City and buy toys for the store. Fowler Brothers really did not carry toys. Richard departed for the city as ordered. Wouldn't you know that the World Series was going on there? Calvin had handed him tickets and told him he should go to the games when the toy-buying was completed. Richard was ecstatic! Well, the toys arrived, but they didn't sell too well. We all wondered what Calvin was going to do about this mistake. He had a plan for that as well. On Christmas Eve, Calvin had all the remaining toy inventory delivered to a local orphanage as their Christmas presents. This was a spectacular double play! This one warmed the hearts of everybody who knew about it. Calvin was having fun and he was my friend!

Calvin had a brother, John Fowler. John liked to drink a bit. He was not too serious about learning the furniture business. I was told that on one Christmas Eve, while celebrating, he went to an orphanage and adopted four children for his wife's Christmas present. I didn't know John, so I cannot fully validate this extraordinary happening. I do know the Fowlers did things on a large scale.

I will end my stories of Calvin Fowler by telling you about my last call on my dear friend. Calvin had been rather sick for several years, suffering with leukemia. We all knew it would be fatal. So I asked his secretary to please call me near the end. I received that call. I hastened to Chattanooga to show my final respects to this extraordinary individual. When I arrived, I found that Calvin was indeed in the hospital and the end was near. I called his lovely wife, Mami, and asked if it would be all right for me to visit him. She said, "Of course. I'll meet you at the hospital and we'll visit together." We headed for Calvin's room — along the Calvin Fowler wing of the hospital, dreading what we would find. As we walked into the room, Calvin spied me and said, "I don't believe my eyes! You don't give up, do you, son! You're here to get an order, aren't you?" Well, with this, I shrank and was so embarrassed. I quickly responded that I knew he was sick and I just wanted to visit him. I told him that this visit was on me. His response, "I don't believe that! You've never made a visit without having something to sell." I felt that I was in real trouble. I looked at Mami and asked if she would explain to her husband that I was there as a friend showing concern. She related this to Calvin. Then Calvin said, "Okay, son, go and get your fabrics and pictures and we'll write an order." I simply could not do this and told him that I couldn't. He said, "I'm in charge of this business, and I'm giving you an order." I knew he was serious, but I still hesitated. A second order came for me to get my bag and fabrics and bring them to his room. With this I slipped out of the room in a daze. I secured my bag and fabrics and looked like a pack-mule going along those long hallways. Everyone was staring at me and wondering what kind of high pressure salesman I must be. I felt awful! I finally walked into his room, and this is what I was greeted with: "I really didn't think you would actually do it." That did me in! He said, "If you really care for me, you would get this stuff out of my room and go to the Reed House and write me a very good order that will last a very long time. You know this is my final order and I want you to do me justice with such an order." I looked at Mami and she responded, "You heard him, and if I were you I'd do it!" After telling Calvin of my love and appreciation for him over these 25 years that I had enjoyed with him, I held his hand and said goodbye. No one could ever believe the distressed and confused feelings I had at this moment. I walked back down those long halls, with everyone staring at me again, to my auto. I went to the hotel in deep sadness, like never before in my life. I first said to myself, *Plato, you just can't do this, it is wrong.* I thought for a very long time and finally realized that I should not let my dear friend down. I wrote quite an order and then didn't know what to do with it. I just couldn't mail the copy to Fowler Brothers because they wouldn't understand. So, I hand-delivered it to the store and tried to explain the circumstances. Much to my surprise, they honored it because Calvin had already called the store and told them that the order was legitimate. Was I relieved!

I spent the night in Chattanooga, and sure enough, Calvin died that night. I stayed around for his very sad funeral, at which the city turned out in large numbers. I had lost a very wonderful friend and customer. My mind flashed back over the unique 25 years of having the opportunity to call on such a marvelous man. Life at Fowler Brothers would never be the same again. One of the great ones had passed away. Never had I received such an order and never would I for the rest of my long career. My dear friend, Calvin, would no longer be around to see what I was made of, and he would not have to wrack his brain to think of some practical joke to play on me.

There is one more final story I must relate, for it had nothing to do with selling and buying. This story has to do with love and feelings. It happened on a Friday afternoon early in my friendship with Calvin.

A Dream to Sell

Calvin said to me, after we had worked out his order, "Son, what in the world are you doing here on a Friday and not home with your lovely bride? I'm going to call her right now and have her fly here, at my expense, and the two of you can spend the weekend with Mami and me." I said, "That is too much, Calvin, however thoughtful you are." He made the call to Betty, and she caught the next flight out to Chattanooga, arriving later that Friday night. Their home, where I had been before, was a tremendous stone structure that Calvin said was built originally by "some of those Coca Cola people." He had had it remodeled, and it was simply beautiful. The bathrooms, especially, were to die for. Betty and I felt like the "Beverly Hills Hillbillies!" The Fowlers entertained us royally, even taking us out to the Fairyland Country Club for dinner on Saturday night. We all had a grand time together. Calvin was Calvin, however, and he played a few tricks on us while we were there. We departed Sunday afternoon, by my auto, for the long drive back to High Point. The memory is today fresh in my mind and will always be. Unfortunately, Betty died a few years later, in 1988, but we talked about that hospitality of Mami and Calvin Fowler many, many times. It truly was a unique experience and put together on the spot, by Calvin. This shows you how caring Calvin was. A true measure of the man! Many, and especially I, never really understood Calvin Fowler. I do know, down deep, he was a very mushy and kind person who always thought of others. He shared his wealth and ran a great furniture operation. He truly was a legend in his time and that legend lives today. There was but one Calvin Fowler, my friend. God rest his happy soul!

CHAPTER 6

In the Trenches
on the Front Line

Henredon

June 30, 1981

Mr. Plato S. Wilson
908 Parkwood Circle
High Point, N.C. 27260

Dear Plato:

This is to advise you that your representation of Henredon and
Schoonbeck as sales representative is hereby terminated, effective
July 6, 1981.

You will receive commissions on all orders from the territory in which
you previously represented Henredon and Schoonbeck currently on file
or received and accepted by the company on or before July 6, 1981, to
be paid to you following shipment of such orders.

Sincerely yours,

William E. Smith

WES/rcm

HENREDON *Fine Furniture*

Plato S. Wilson
July 3, 1981

To My Devoted Customers:

I have written you many letters and issued some 31 year-end "report cards." Today I received my report card from Henredon. As a result, this will be my last letter to you.

It all started for me 35 years ago in the foundation ditches of Henredon's first factory building. It ended for me in Asheville, NC yesterday. I was where I loved to be — in the trenches on the front line. Being a traveling furniture salesman has been my joy and life! I have enjoyed it more than you can imagine! And, it has been good to me!

Effective Monday, July 6, 1981, I will no longer be your Henredon representative. Henredon has seen fit to terminate me for no stated reason. I will have to say I am shocked.

However, I feel better for having had such wonderful friends and customers to share my many years. You have always shown me your very best in every way. I have tried to express my gratitude to you over the years, but have always felt this gratitude really never came through. Today, please know that I love you, respect you, and am very happy to call you my genuine friend. We are family!

I will miss you, and I trust you will miss me! Friends never get too far from each other. I trust we can keep our long friendships in good repair! I will try.

Time has not allowed me any future plans. I will have time for this later, I'm sure, much time! If you have any ideas, let me know.

Even though national baseball is on strike now, I want you to know that they did play in Mudville last night and "Mighty Casey has struck out!" But — what do they say? — "The ballgame is not over until the fat lady sings!" Well, I certainly hope she stays quiet for a long time to come!

With all my love, thanks, and expectations for your continued success, I remain –

Very truly yours,
Plato S. Wilson

A Dream to Sell

The previous letters describe what it is like to be "in the trenches on the front line" in the selling world. Having an excellent sales record does not, necessarily, assure one of a secure job. Later in this chapter, I will give you an explanation of those letters.

For now, I would like to relate some of the more interesting events that happened around me as I progressed upward and onward in my sales career. We have all heard the famous quote, "The course of love and war never runs smoothly." That quote overflows into the business world as well. I am getting ready to tell you more about the "overflow."

Most of my career in the furniture industry was fantastic. I had so much fun that I could not believe they sent me monthly checks! I've often said that there was not enough money to pay for the fun and joy that I had in my career. To explain the 18 speeding tickets that I received in my 44 years of traveling, I always said that my message was so good that I couldn't wait to get to the next account.

As a rookie salesman I worked for Heritage-Henredon Furniture Company. This was a dynamic combination. Heritage Furniture Company was headed up by Elliott Wood, and they made the upholstered line and occasional tables while Henredon Furniture Industries made the bedroom and dining room furniture. They split the advertising cost and used a common sales force. They developed complementary lines of furniture that gave their salesmen a chance to double their income. Everyone thought it was a great idea. The two dynamic leaders were opposite — Elliott Wood was high-fashion, good-looking and the best salesmen that I ever knew; Henry Wilson, on the other hand, was a very plain vanilla wrapper who was a genius in business and finance. They were two very good leaders in their own ways. Henry, while president of Drexel Furniture Company, had personally bought stock in the fledgling Heritage Furniture Company with a dream of merging Drexel and Heritage together in the future. When Henry was no longer with Drexel, the dream became to combine, in name only, Heritage and Henredon. The problem developed when success came to the combination. Jealousy occurred between these two very strong leaders. Everyone could see the clash coming! What actually set it off was this: Elliott was an avid bird hunter and planned to acquire land and build a hunting lodge and stock it with birds and ducks. He planned to use Heritage Furniture Company profits and also the Heritage Furniture employees' pension funds, giving them stock for the use of their money. Well, Henry Wilson hit the ceiling because Heritage Furniture had never paid any dividends to their stockholders of whom Henry was one. The tension mounted.

The following story is the best account of what happened next, to the extent of my memory. The plot thickened in late October 1956 when Mr. A.C. Chaffee, who owned most, if not all, of Morganton Furniture Company, decided to sell this company because of his age. Mr. Chaffee called Henry Wilson to see if he or Henredon wanted to buy his company. Henry told Mr. Chaffee that they did not. Then Mr. Chaffee asked Henry if he would, at a price, evaluate his company. Henry reluctantly said he would try to do so. Henry studied the operation and in doing so thought it might, after all, be desirable for Henredon to buy. Henry then went to see his partner at Heritage. Henry had a plan: Heritage would manufacture a lower price upholstered line to go with the lower priced Morganton Furniture wood furniture. He suggested to Elliott a purchase price for Morganton Furniture. Elliott thought this was an excellent plan and told Henry that he should proceed. Henry went back home, called Mr. Chaffee and told him that the deal was on. Mr. Chaffee agreed on the price and told Henry he had the purchase. Earlier, Mr. Robert Huffman of Drexel

Furniture Company, who wanted to put Drexel in the upholstery business, had approached Elliott Wood about Heritage breaking away from Henredon and merging with Drexel. Elliott had turned him down by saying he needed to think long and hard about this.

Now the fireworks were about to begin! On Henry's departure after telling Elliott the price he and Mr. Chaffee had agreed on for the sale of Morganton Furniture, Elliott called Mr. Robert Huffman at Drexel to tell him that he would be interested in merging Heritage into Drexel with two stipulations: (1) Drexel would buy Morganton Furniture Company for Elliott to run; (2) Elliott would be made president of Drexel Furniture Company as well. Mr. Huffman agreed to both requests. Mr. Huffman called Mr. Chaffee and offered him approximately one million dollars more than Henry Wilson was to pay. Mr. Chaffee, a most honorable man, was in a mess! He could not lose the extra million dollars. Mr. Chaffee called Henry Wilson on a Sunday night and told him that he had to back out on their deal, explaining to Henry that Drexel had offered a million dollars more to buy his company. Henry told Mr. Chaffee that he should take the larger price from Drexel. Henry Wilson did not have any idea what was happening behind the scenes.

On Monday morning, the next day, Elliott Wood appeared at Henry Wilson's office at Henredon, announcing that the two of them should buy each other's shares in Heritage Furniture and Henredon Furniture. Elliott announced that Heritage was merging with Drexel and that Mr. Huffman was buying Morganton Furniture for them. Henry now knew why he had lost the deal to buy Morganton Furniture from Mr. Chaffee!

A few days later, on Halloween, Ralph Edwards, the sales manager of Henredon (also, the "RE" in Henredon), was so upset over what was happening to Heritage-Henredon Furniture Company that he telephoned Mr. Robert Huffman of Drexel Furniture Company to give him a piece of his mind on his role as a spoiler. Ralph became so animated that he died of a heart attack with the phone in his hand. How tragic.

I was traveling and was in Fayetteville, NC when I received a telephone call from Betty, telling me of the death of Ralph Edwards. I immediately returned home to High Point to get the proper clothes for my sales manager's funeral, which was to be held in Morganton. While I was packing, Betty brought me the afternoon *High Point Enterprise* newspaper. On the front page on the right side was a picture of Ralph Edwards and an account of his death. On the left side was a picture of Mr. Schoonbeck Sr., president of the Grand Rapids Schoonbeck Company, who had died on the same day that Mr. Edwards had died. I tore off the front page and tossed it in my suitcase.

All of our Heritage-Henredon national salesmen, 12 in all, gathered in Morganton for our boss's funeral. Immediately after the funeral, I gave Henry Wilson the newspaper page that I had in my coat pocket. I told Henry that there was a good possibility he could acquire the Schoonbeck Company, to replace Heritage, to manufacture our upholstery line. Henry Wilson called a meeting of the sales force to convene on the front porch of the local Caldwell Hotel.

One has to understand how fragile Henredon was at this time. It had started from scratch less than ten years earlier. My personal sales were 80 percent Heritage and 20 percent Henredon. Henry Wilson knew this fact, so he had to show his leadership immediately. Henry also knew that the sales force didn't like the salary/bonus compensation plan that we were under at Heritage - Henredon. At the hotel, he opened with these remarks: "I want and need you fellows to stay with Henredon. We want to offer you a straight commission compensation. That commission will be five percent; however, we know your expenses are going to be heavy as a percentage of what you can make with Henredon alone, so we will pay you seven percent until we all make the transition, then it will drop back to five percent. In addition, I want you all to know that we will begin today to find a factory to replace Heritage. We will spend what it takes to be the best quality manufacturer in the country." This was the most outward determination that I had ever witnessed coming from the normally modest man. We believed him and we signed on with him.

Back at Heritage, we heard that Elliott Wood had promised to Drexel that he could deliver the current sales force. Elliott was in trouble after Henry's remarks at the hotel. All of us salesmen shortly received letters from Elliott Wood allowing ten days to decide which of the two companies we would choose to work for in the future. Evidently, Elliott was not aware of Henry's great proposition made to us. As it turned out, Henry did not extend his offer to two of our salesmen for one reason or another. Ten out of twelve wasn't bad for Henredon in their fragile state. Elliot must have felt betrayed.

Already knowing that I would stay with my loyal and trusted friend, Henry, I went in person to see Elliott Wood and to thank him for the great contribution he had made to my career and to also tell him that I would be working for Henredon in the future. His remarks to me will always be remembered: "Plato, I'm not surprised as to your decision. Henredon needs salesmen like you if they ever hope to succeed. We really do not need high-powered salesmen in that our line is pre-sold." I took his left-handed complement that I was, in his eyes, a real salesman and went forward knowing that my future looked easier than I had planned. I always like to compete with a pre-sold line.

Thus, the fireworks ended. Everyone had adjustments to make and much work to do. There were mixed emotions, of course, because we had enjoyed very much having worked for a winning combination of two outstanding leaders and the best products made in America. Life goes on and we were happy to be in step with Henry Wilson!

Henry Wilson did follow up on his promise of buying an upholstery factory to replace Heritage. After some negotiations, he was able to merge with, guess who, the Schoonbeck Company. Jack Campbell, who ran North Carolina Schoonbeck, was a big help in bringing this about. After the merger, I was able to secure my good friend Sue Burns to come with Schoonbeck. Sue was the best upholstery designer in the country and was working at the time for Heritage Furniture. I was also able to secure some more key Heritage production people for the Schoonbeck Company. Henry was thinking big and wanted additional production and expanded factories at the new upholstery factory. He was making good on the late October 1957 promise that he made to us on the front porch of the Caldwell Hotel. We had enormous growth both at Henredon and at Schoonbeck. For national advertisements and for simplistic reasons, the name of our combined company simply became Henredon.

In a very short time, we were doing very well with Henredon. As salesmen, we were back making money on the five percent commission that Henry had promised. Bill Smith, a fellow salesman in Chicago, was brought in to replace the late Ralph Edwards as sales manager. We had turned the corner and everyone seemed very happy.

The actual truth of the matter was that we had taken much of the market share from our competitor, Heritage-Drexel Furniture Company. Henredon's entire sales force was simply better than theirs! A humorous story made its way back to me as a result of our success. During one of the Heritage-Drexel sales meetings, prior to a High Point Furniture Market, their sales manager sat his salesmen down in a room and asked a question to each: "Why do you think our competitor, Henredon, is doing so well at our expense?" Each salesman had one excuse or another. When the question was asked to Claude Russell, a friend and fellow Morgantonian (and my direct competitor), his answer was, "You guys don't know what competition is! I am up against Plato Wilson, who doesn't drink or smoke and works twelve to fifteen hours a day! He even adopts his children because he's on the road constantly!" I suppose this is very immodest for me to tell this about Claude, but there's some truth in what he said. I have always been very serious about selling.

Then I received some surprises over the next 10-to-15 years. These came in the way of territorial reductions. Each of them reduced my territory by usually one-half. These hurt to the bone.

The first reduction came when my sales reached approximately two and one-half million dollars. I could not believe the letter from Bill Smith that announced that I would not need to travel the state of Tennessee and part of Arkansas. I was surprised that my friend Henry Wilson would agree to this action. I loved to travel Tennessee and had super clients there. I had an idea! Since I felt as qualified as anyone Henredon could hire to replace me in the state of Tennessee, I decided to make myself a resume, picture, and recommendations from all the key stores in the state and submit this to my friend and president of Henredon. I called Henry to make a firm appointment. Henry said that I didn't need an appointment, as usual, and for me to just drop by whenever I wanted to. I said that I really did want a time that I could discuss something very important with him. I went to the appointment at the proper time and tossed my complete resume on his desk. He looked at it and discovered that I was applying for the same job that I had had in the state of Tennessee. He laughed and stated that he had never heard of such a thing. He allowed that I was better qualified than anyone he knew, but that he had to support his sales manager, Bill Smith. I didn't get the job back, but at least I let them know I had a mind and courage.

The last reduction had a tragic ending as well. This time, I did not receive a letter or memo. I received a telephone call from Bill Smith, my sales manager. He requested that I drive to Morganton, and meet with him and president John Collett. The appointment was at 5:30 p.m.

on a certain date. I became very alarmed as this seemed serious to me. I appeared at the proper time and was told of the reduction of my territory. They both told me that I was just making too much money, in fact, more than they were receiving. I was already very upset, so I said that I had a simple solution to their problem: Don't reduce my income, just simply give both of yourselves raises. After all, you are both top management! Well, this did not go over very well at all. Both John and Bill seemed shocked that they needed help in running Henredon, especially from a lowly salesman. The reduction stuck, and I went away to heal myself. By this time, my original sales territory of three and one-half states was down to Western North Carolina! So much for working 18 hours a day and succeeding big time! As bad as these five territory reductions were, there was even worse to come. Whoever said that trench fighting on the front lines was easy, especially when the enemy was within your own company?

I was able to right my ship after all those reductions and come back with excellent sales and even reach new highs in my volume of sales. I did this with even more effort, longer days and smarter selling. Then, suddenly on June 30, 1981, I was fired! The last shoe had fallen. This letter and my reply are printed at the opening of this chapter. I will endeavor to tell you how it all played out.

As you can see, it all started with a seven-line letter giving me a seven-day notice and was over the Fourth of July weekend, with no explanation as to why I was relieved. I'd say that this was real "fireworks on the Fourth of July." I was devastated because my life for 35 years was totally Henredon! My dream of selling furniture for Henry Wilson had begun even further back, in 1942, thirty-nine years ago.

Henredon appointed Edward Phifer, a good friend and fellow Morgantonian, to be my successor in my former territory. After his tenure with Henredon, Edward went on to help found E.J. Victor Furniture Company in Morganton, NC. Much success has come to this high quality furniture manufacturing company, both casegoods and upholstery.

This is how it all happened: I was traveling to the far west of my territory when I stopped by Henredon in Morganton to pick up catalogs, price lists and supplies. I was about to depart when my good friend Roy, who was in charge of all the mail, said to me, "Where are you going?" I told him that I was heading west to Asheville and beyond. He told me that he thought I should go home and read my mail. An alarm bell went off in my head. Why should Roy tell me to go home? What did he know? I dismissed the alarm bell and went on to Asheville for my appointments the next morning. It was a rather sleepless night for me. I made my first call on Bruce Shipley the next morning. I could not get this off my mind, so about 11 a.m. I decided to call my dear friend, Jack Campbell, president of Schoonbeck. I was told that Jack was out for lunch. Well, I could never remember Jack going to lunch at 11 o'clock! I called him again at 2 p.m., and he was still out to lunch. Something was not ringing true in all of this. At about 3 p.m. I finally reached Jack and asked him if there was anything I should know about this letter Roy told me that I was receiving. He simply said, "Plato, I think you should go home and read your mail." I then said to Jack, "Jack, am I being fired?" He replied, "I think you should go home and read your mail." Now real bells went off throughout my mind! I still had one more appointment with my good friend, Chuck England at Morrison's Furniture in Asheville. I half-heartedly made the call. I was really not in the proper state of mind to give a sales presentation. I told Chuck that I suspected that I had been fired from Henredon. He was about as shocked as I was. He asked if he could drive me to High Point. I thanked him but said that I was okay. I departed for home, arriving at approximately 6 p.m.

The house was empty since Betty was away for a six-week trip out West, our son Craig was in summer school at Duke and Susan was away at camp as a counselor. I went to the mailbox and happened to remember that I had forwarded our mail to our little summer cottage at Gingercake. We were in the process of moving there for the summer. Of course, there was no mail in my mailbox, because it had been sent to the mountains. I immediately called Jack Campbell at his home to see if he would enlighten me as to what the letter stated. I spoke with his wife, Ruth, and she said Jack had already had dinner but had taken a walk. I told her to have Jack call me at my home in High Point just as soon as he returned from his walk. I waited and waited. At about 9 p.m., Jack returned the call. I again asked him what was in the letter and if I had been possibly fired. In a very weakened voice that was full of stress he said, "I think you have been fired." I asked him why, and he said, "Plato, I think you should go to the mountains tomorrow and read your letter." I was in no mood to wait till tomorrow. I thanked him for telling me the contents of the letter. I immediately got into the car and drove for 2 hours to see the letter. I arrived at Gingercake at about midnight to find not one letter, but two identical ones. Bill Smith had sent two letters, one to High Point and the other on to our mountain address. It was not double fun reading these letters.

Unable to sleep, I rose and went down to our barn and saddled my horse, Rex, and we took off into the Pisgah Forest. We watched the sun come up over Gingercake Mountain. It was one of the lowest moments of my life. While riding, I decided to call my good friend and fraternity brother from Duke days, Carlton Fleming, one of the best lawyers in the South. I suspected there might be a lawsuit in all of this somewhere. I returned from the horseback ride to our cottage and called Carlton in Charlotte. He said, "Come on down." I arrived there about 1 p.m., and we talked all afternoon. He asked me a thousand questions and finally told me that there was a lawsuit there on the basis of discrimination. He said he would handle the case and charge me a $200,000 legal fee and that I could collect a gross amount of one million dollars. He allowed this would take a year and a half and that I would become a bitter person as a result of the trial. He then told me that if he were I, he would take my excellent sales record and get myself another better job and forget this whole mess. I accepted this good advice on the spot. I asked him what I owed him for his time, and his answer was, "Nothing. You have been punished too much already." I thanked him and departed Charlotte for High Point where I would begin to notify our two children and write to all of my accounts before Henredon advised them of my termination. I decided not to tell Betty about this bad news until she returned from her long awaited trip out West. I didn't want to rain on her parade!

I called Craig at Duke summer school, and he met me in High Point, trying to console me and helping me with the letter to my dealers. His birthday was July 5th, and this was not a good birthday present for him. Susan was alerted at Camp Yonahlossee near Blowing Rock. I asked her if she still had her job there as counselor, and she replied, "Sure Dad, what's up?" I told her that she was the only one in the family who had a job because I had lost mine! I reported to her that Craig and I were going to the mountain cottage and Craig's birthday was Saturday, July 5th. She said she would bake him a birthday cake (her first ever) on reaching the cottage. On her way to the cottage she decided to pick up my favorite donuts. In her haste, she had skidded her new Volkswagen convertible into a ditch but was able to drive on to meet us. By the time we all met at the cottage, she had baked Craig's cake, and what a cake it was! She had run out of icing, and one side was plain, so she just placed that un-iced side against the wall. We all had good laughs over this, our first since the matter of my being fired began.

Betty called in from her travels on the weekends. We talked about everything but my being fired. The three of us back home began to think about how we would break the bad news to her on her return home. One weekend when we were all together, we put ourselves in three separate rooms with the task of coming up with a script that would be used to advise our mother and wife of what had happened in her absence. The winning script was, "Betty, we've got good news for you! You don't have to file acknowledgments and invoices anymore (a job she disliked). Daddy is no longer with Henredon!" She was to arrive in Winston-Salem, so we picked her favorite restaurant there, Ryan's, and made reservations for four. We were going to have a fun dinner and then during dessert and coffee I would use the selected script. It all went as scheduled. We all looked at Betty while I repeated the rehearsed speech. On hearing this, we noted one teardrop from her right eye and that was it. She immediately said, "That's fine, we will do better than ever." Then the four of us celebrated our freedom, at last, from such an un-appreciating company. We all felt a real relief. We would discover there was life after 40 years of devotion to Henredon. I was sincerely glad that Henry Wilson was not there to see the end of the dream he had given me in 1942, thirty-nine years ago!

I could not believe how fast the news of my being fired traveled. After all, I was just a salesman, not even another pretty face in the crowd. Hundreds of friends telephoned me their condolences; letters poured in from everywhere; friends and competitors came to see me in person. I could not believe all the attention. After all, I had been fired! I believe my biggest surprise came with over 53 job offers, in an array of companies — two to run major factories. I decided to honor all of these offers and arranged for appointments with all of them, whether I was really interested or not. I did not want to be ungrateful. It took me three months to complete this process. I never learned so much and met so many wonderful people as I did in these three months. Normally, competitors in the furniture industry do not invite other people in the industry to come into their domains. It was a chance of a lifetime, and I'll have to say, not only was the experience education-al but it was enjoyable. I left the door open, as to my answer on the job offer, until I had completed all the interviews.

In the course of these interviews, my retail friends told me that I was a good match for Henkel-Harris Furniture in Winchester, VA. I knew they were small but had an A-1 product. It so happened their salesman of many years had just retired, and they had a waiting list of applicants of over 200. I would be, actually 203 on the list if I applied! I found out that Mary Henkel, founder and owner, and Carlton Mallory, vice president of sales, were actually in High Point, planning their showroom for the fall of 1981. I called them at their showroom to ask if I could visit them. They consented, and I immediately went there. I showed them my resume to which I had attached my lifetime sales graph. Mary Henkel took a look and said, "I can't hire you because you sell too much furniture!" I said, "Mrs. Henkel, are you saying that you want to hire a bad salesman?" She laughed and told me she would think about that. The key for my actually getting the job was the two telephone calls Mary Henkel made. One was to her confidant, Henry Foscue of High Point, who said to her, "Mary, can you really hire Plato Wilson? If you can, hire him before noon today!" The other phone call was to Jack Campbell, the president of the Schoonbeck Company, a division of Henredon, for whom I had worked. She wanted to know why I was fired. Jack told Mary, "Plato is an excellent person and salesperson. It was not his fault he was fired. You would do well if you hired him now." Mary called me to invite me to visit her factory in Winchester, VA and I did!

What a factory — not huge but clean as could be and with all new machinery. It resembled a hospital, located in a residential area on a very large tract of land. All the employees (maybe 1/3 women) loved the family and their jobs. Well, between Mary and Carlton Mallory, they gave me the job! It was one of the happiest days of my life. I had the best eight years of my career with them and was able to triple my income. Things were beginning to look up for me. All that ends well

Chapter 6 – In the Trenches on the Front Line

is well! You never know which friend might help you out so be nice to them all. My friendships with Henry Foscue and Jack Campbell were well and alive. I shall never forget their kind help. I was reminded of the lumberman on the West Coast who went broke 11 times and finally coined the now famous quote: "Be nice to the people on the way up because they are the same ones you meet on the way down!"

As you can see, life in sales is not without pitfalls. A sales career is for survivors and persistence. The key for success is to stay flexible, keep your sales record tip top, always keep your personal reputation and morals without any question. People who wear honest white hats always win! That should be good news for those who choose this noble profession.

In October 1981 I resumed my interrupted sales career. I was so happy and hopeful. On my first day in the Henkel-Harris showroom, however, I received a shock. I had been used to a 40,000-square foot, state-of-the-art showroom. Well, this new showroom was tiny and pretty shabbily decorated. I could not reconcile the state of the factory and their showroom. I called my wife and told her I had made a mistake in joining Henkel-Harris Furniture. Their showroom looked like an elephant grave yard. By the end of my first day (1 a.m. the next day), while still working and writing orders, I called Betty back and told her that I had not made a mistake. I had written more business in one day than I had written in entire markets at Henredon. At this market, the company had introduced solid walnut to go with their solid cherry and mahogany. No one could believe they could offer American black walnut since walnut was so rare. Well, somehow, Henkel-Harris had found a reliable source. My first customer was Whitley's in the little town of Zebulon near Raleigh. The buyer, Amos Estes, came in and could not wait to begin to buy. Typically, he told me to give him six suites in all three woods! We went through the small showroom with the same quantities. The order must have totaled over $150,000. It went on all day. I could see why they didn't waste money on the showroom. This was the opposite of a graveyard — it was Heaven!

I had been told, on accepting the job, that I could have a million-dollar allotment. In three weeks, I had sold this amount and called Mr. Mallory, the vice president of sales at Henkel-Harris, to find out what I should I do the rest of the year? He simply said, "Keep working, I will give you another million dollars to sell." I was pleased to charge ahead. Never again in my career with Henkel-Harris were allotments mentioned. I finally finished my eight years in the $8,000,000 to $10,000,000 per year shipments range. How nice they were to me.

Now, back to routine traveling with this fine "bag of furniture." In selling wood furniture only, one can travel much faster and with less effort, as opposed to having to deal with upholstered sales with all the frames and 1,500 fabrics. I could work three to four towns a day, with good organization. This required staying up half the night to organize records and write suggested orders. My backlog of orders to be shipped over a year's period was $5,093,842 as of April 1, 1989, my largest backlog. I did not have a computer, so I made hand printouts, and continued to book the next quarter. Ninety-eight percent of the buyers accepted the suggested new orders. I made a photocopy of the dealer's backlog and his new order. He then had worksheets to sell into. He was never out of furniture. Most of my fellow salesmen didn't go to this trouble, so they came up short and let their stores run out and had to wait a very long time for stock and special orders. Experience is a good teacher!

Back in 1951, my first real goal for my annual sales was to be able to sell one million dollars. It grew in 44 years to be a goal of shipments of $10,000,000 which I finally hit. Well, on a very lucky day near the end of my career, the stars lined up and I was able to book over one million dollars of orders in one 24-hour period. It all happened this way: One morning I left a proposed order with my good friend and account, John Young, of Young's Furniture in High Point. John was out, but I was assured he would review and enhance the order if I would stop by the next day and pick it up. I motored up to Hickory that day to call on my super friend and buyer, Larry Hendricks, of the Country Shop. Larry was busy that afternoon, but he told me to get my suggestions together after consulting his inventory. I hung around all afternoon doing this. Larry then told me that we should go to dinner together and work on the order after dinner. Larry is a very, very slow eater (contrary to everything else he does), so we didn't get back to work until about 9:30 p.m. We worked, and he bought about twice as much as I had suggested. We finished about 12:30 a.m. I headed for a motel in Hickory so I could write this up while my notes were fresh. At 3:30 a.m., I totaled the order, and it amounted to $550,000.00. With four hours of sleep, I went back to High Point to see John Young. He was not there, but his secretary handed me an envelope and said this was for me. I hastily opened it, and much to my surprise there was a computer-generated order for Henkel-Harris for $490,000. My dream of a lifetime had come to reality — in one day I was able to book $1,040,000. What a day! I was not tired at all. I couldn't wait to get to my next account. When you're hot, you're hot — I was on a roll! I'm sorry to say that my next day was not that kind of day, but I had had my dream, once-in-a-lifetime experience. I had fully forgotten the bad experience that I had had at Henredon. Good sales are a cure for many ailments. I had been in training for 42 years for this extraordinary one day, but I still had two years to go to complete my career.

I had many, many fine buyers to work with in my career. Many had gotten better with time — same as I had. Each buyer does it his or her way and is unique. It is not really fair to single out the best one or two buyers, but I must recognize two that have the track record to prove their being the best. One is Boyce Grindstaff of Grindstaff's, Forest

City, NC. He is fast, accurate, has excellent taste and is a true Christian man. I had the privilege of calling on his father first and then Boyce right out of UNC, Chapel Hill. I knew from the beginning he was a winner and a first-class owner, buyer and salesperson. Boyce, his family and associates have and still are doing a fantastic job for their clients. The other top notch buyer is Larry Hendricks, owner of Boyles Furniture. Larry is in many ways quite different from Boyce. They have different approaches to success. Larry is the most courageous of all buyers I've known. He thinks very large, not only in buying but in the vast number of stores he's expanded into. He's very good at it all. He loves to manage a dozen balls in the air at one time. Boyce Grindstaff has but one store and does much of the selling himself, with fantastic results. Both men are excellent friends. Even 12 years after I retired in 1990, I stay in touch with them and continue to cheer them on — as if they needed my help! "The cream rises to the top." So hurrah for the trench fighters on the front lines, whoever they may be. They make good things happen!

CHAPTER 7

The Seminars

Most of my good decisions in my career stemmed from good ol' common sense. The solutions just seemed to be logical and simple. A good example of this was my idea of mass training of all the salespersons who worked in my retail stores and who were responsible, ultimately, for moving the product into the homes. I had often said, in sales meetings across my territory, that in the long chain from the tree, through the factories, into the retail stores and to the final salesperson, it is their mammoth task to tell the whole convincing story of the worth of the factory and the product to the home owner. What a responsibility! Most all of these retail sales people or decorators simply did not have the adequate knowledge to do their jobs effectively. Many of the factory reps tried, feebly, to hold sales meetings but came up short. One of the problems that I discovered was that they lacked the confidence or status to think that they could talk to a brain surgeon and his wife about products. Not that these salespeople were not excellent persons; they simply didn't have the facts from the first-hand information. I saw the need and formulated the answer. They needed to come to the factories and see and learn about what they were trying to sell. I would put on seminars at the factories and mass-train them, let them tour and talk with the craftsmen, meet our fabric people and our lumber people, tour our beautiful showrooms, meet and have dinner with our entire management team and finally hear "the gospel according to Plato Wilson."

Conversations in their store, after attending seminars, went like this:

The customer: *"What brand of furniture should we buy?"*

Salesperson: *"If you want something that is real quality and a good value, I would recommend Henredon."*

Customer: *"Why do you say this?"*

Salesperson: *"Recently, I visited their factory for training and even had dinner with their president. I came away as a real believer! I believe you would enjoy their products for many years. They are first-class people."*

Now the salesperson had confidence and knowledge and some prestige — all qualities that were missing before the seminar. It was working for everyone: the factory, me as their representative, the owner of the store, the salesperson and finally the consumer. My personal sales soared after these events. The commonsense solution of filling a void was working.

The planning of the seminars had a three-month lead time in preparation. I had to engage the factory personnel, management, and various participants, prepare letters to the stores, etc. I did this on weekends so as not to distract from my constant traveling. So that all retail salespersons could come, I scheduled two sessions in the week-long event. The first group arrived on Sunday afternoon, and my wife and I had a giant cocktail party for them at our home. The seminar began promptly Monday morning and ended with a big dinner that night. On Tuesday the seminar continued, with graduation late in the afternoon. Then the first participants departed for their homes. On Tuesday night the second group arrived and we repeated the first session. In this manner, all salespeople from one store came, and the store would not be without salesmen at any time.

You can imagine how expensive this was since all High Point accommodations were free of charge to the participants. All they had to pay was their transportation to and from the seminar, which their stores usually paid. The hotels, food and other expenses totaled, usually, approximately $25,000 for the full week. I imposed on Henredon and Schoonbeck to pay for two-thirds of this expense and I paid the rest. I tried to hold these events every other year, but a few times I did them annually. Since I was the only factory representative who offered this schooling, the events were very popular. The participants could excel in selling our products, and also could use the technical experience and sales training to sell other brands as well. To my surprise, I did not know of any other furniture factories that even tried to duplicate these seminars — at least while I represented Henredon. Later, after I was fired, Henredon hired a special person whose job it was to do this on a national basis. Later Drexel copied the plan, but for 25 years mine was the only show in town. I believe this was one of the best things I did for my retail friends. My sales soared and I looked much better than I really was. As it turned out, it all reminded me of the story of Tom Sawyer who interested many in helping him paint a very long white fence. One person can only do so much, but an army can achieve the ultimate!

Word somehow leaked out about my seminars, and I received many calls from other industries that wanted me to explain the details to them so they could duplicate them. Of course, I sent all a packet of letters and agendas. They seemed to be grateful. A footnote: The gold Cross pens that I gave away at the many seminars turned into my personal responsibility to replace those that were lost or stolen. No decent retail salesperson would be without a Cross pen that had "Henredon" engraved on it. They were a status symbol and flattering to me. I received many telephone calls requesting another gold pen due to loss. I finally bought a large quantity, had them engraved, and carried them with me as I traveled. I must have given away 2,000 or more of them. That was a very small price to pay for loyalty. I also had a supply of refills for their convenience.

There is another footnote to the seminars: Since my retirement in 1990, I have been honored to give national sales meetings for big furniture manufacturers — some with more than a hundred salesmen. What a thrill for me to get another chance at bat! The fees weren't bad either! I think my ability to do public speaking was developed in the over 40 years of teaching adult Sunday school classes in my church. I'm afraid that I learned more than they did. Four hours of study was required to produce a 40-minute Sunday school lesson.

CHAPTER 8

My Excellent Good Friend
Rhett Jackson

A Dream to Sell

I first met Rhett Jackson at my first furniture market in Chicago in 1951. He was from the big city of North, SC population 500. Nervous as I was, I sold him — or he bought — a pretty good order. This meeting was the beginning of a life-long close friendship. Along with Rhett and his wife Betty Culler Jackson, there was also Betty's brother Bill Culler, and his girlfriend, Martha. I asked the four of them to be my guests for dinner at the Edgewater Beach Hotel, a little north of Chicago and a fine place to go in the summer. We became better acquainted and in the course of dinner, Bill Culler asked Martha if she would marry him while they were in Chicago. She said yes, and they were married in Bill's hotel room. How's that for quick reactions?

I must tell you about North, SC. It's located approximately 25 miles south of Columbia on Hwy. 21 — just a wide place in the road with one stoplight. This is the town where Betty and Bill Culler grew up. Their father and mother were exceptional people who owned much of the town. Their names were Kathleen and Isadore. Isadore was a real piece of work. He was involved in everything from furniture, candy-making, punch boards, real estate, farming and even a cemetery. He had been in the state legislature with a most colorful record. When Betty and Rhett married, after a short career in the appliance business in Holly Hill, SC, they joined Isadore in his furniture business there in North. Incidentally, the world famous singer Eartha Kitt called North her home, as well.

It was a real coincidence that only a few months earlier in April 1951 my new bride, Betty Cashion, and I spent the first night of our honeymoon in Denmark, SC, just a few miles south of North. The reason was that no hotel or motel rooms were available in Columbia due to the Easter weekend, and every soldier at Fort Jackson either had his mother, wife or girlfriend in town. Little did I know that in a very short

Chapter 8 – My Excellent Good Friend Rhett Jackson

time I would meet my life's friend, Rhett. Life is that way, sometimes.

A little more about Isadore. Isadore, was a magician who traveled all over the U.S. to attend conventions. At these conventions, he had met Mr. Coke Cecil of High Point, NC — also a magician. Small world! Isadore had collected a large number of old, large paper bills known as "big money." He taped them together end to end and rolled them up and placed a rubber band around them. He took this big money with him to a Philadelphia magician's convention. On checking out of his hotel there, he just tossed the roll of big money up on the counter and told the cashier to just cut off what he needed. He also told him that he was trying to spend this old money before he started on his new money. You can imagine the expression on the city slicker's face! This was Isadore, at his normal best. Kathleen Culler had to be a saint to put up with Rhett's father-in-law, Isadore. She truly was and is today, a first-class lady. Kathleen Culler still lives in North and still drives her Oldsmobile as she approaches 100. What a beautiful lady — Isadore would be so proud of her. On Wednesday afternoon, when all retail stores closed, the Cullers would have all of us traveling salesmen over to their home for a cookout. You can bet that every salesmen in driving distance made it to these cookouts! Much fun and many friendships developed.

Rhett and Betty raised their daughter Kay and son Jim there in North. On one occasion, having been invited to their home for pot luck supper, I shall never forget a conversation Rhett had with Jim who was about 10 years old, Rhett said, "Jim, have you prepared your lessons yet?" Jim replied, "Yes, dad, I've prepared my lessons, but I haven't studied yet." There's no wonder that Jim went on to Davidson College and graduated with honors and then on to University of Virginia to receive an honors law degree. He later became the assistant attorney general of the State of Alaska, where he still lives. Kay went on to be a wonderful mother and a beautiful lady.

Since this chapter is about my friend Rhett Jackson, I need to tell you more about him. Rhett and Larry were identical twins born in Florence, SC — the sons of a railroad man. They ran a swap on the girls they dated and as far as I know, no one knew the difference! Both were officers in the Navy. Rhett was a cheerleader for the University of South Carolina while attending and graduating there. Larry was at one time president of Lander College. Both were Christians and Methodists. Two very outstanding people that made their family very proud. Larry and Rhett were over six feet tall and very handsome. Rhett was a study in surprises. He could look like a model when he was all dressed up, and then he could surprise you by coming out with blue jeans, plaid shirt, red suspenders and some kooky hat with brogan shoes. He was at his best when he bought a surplus red caboose from the railroad, in honor of his father, and had it placed on his man-made fishing lake near Columbia. I would join him and some of his retail salesmen and enjoy fishing, cookouts and just sitting in the red caboose. What memories!

Rhett and Betty came to visit us at our little mountain cottage at Gingercake one time. Rhett said, "While we are having fun, Plato, why don't you get your photos and fabrics out and we'll write an order. I did, and he bought a truckload of upholstered furniture, much to my surprise. Another time he was in our High Point showroom and asked, "What would it cost me to buy the entire upholstered showroom samples?" I told him that I didn't know, but I would find out. Well, much to my surprise he bought the whole showroom, rented the steel building at the South Carolina Fairgrounds in Columbia and had a sale. He was successful. Another great surprise! He taught me what imagination is all about.

There is an incident that occurred at midnight when the sale ended at the steel building at the fairground. Most salesmen would head to their motels to sleep. I had a different idea. The next day I had the long drive to Hilton Head, SC, not to sell furniture, but to collect for some that I had sold before. This long trip was going to eat up a lot of the daylight, so I decided to drive there that night. All salesmen quickly learn that you cannot sell anything to an account and collect money on the same visit. So it was not going to be profitable on this visit. It would mean that I was only helping my home offices. There are some factories that charge any bad debts back against the salesmen's commissions, but mine did not, and I wanted to keep our policy by helping them collect their debts.

The fireworks began for me when I reached Hilton Head. It was now about 4 a.m., and I was really tired and sleepy as I approached a roundabout near my destination hotel, where, of course, I did not have reservations due to my abrupt decision to travel there. Instead of going all around the roundabout, I chose to short cut it and missed half of the circle and went directly to the road to the hotel. There was no traffic at all, so I thought that there was no danger to anyone. Wouldn't you know, there in the bushes was a patrolman waiting. He pulled me over and inquired if I realized that I had broken the law. I replied that I realized this, but also realized that at 4 a.m. and with no traffic whatsoever, I thought I had not caused any danger. I also told him that he and I were the only people in the world who knew about this. He shook his head and laughed and said that I was probably right and let me go. I soon reached the hotel to check in for a few hours of sleep. I first asked the sleepy desk clerk if he had a room, which he admitted that he did. A salesman always inquires about the rates before signing in. Very matter-of-factly, he told me the rate was $175 per day. With this remark, I exploded and told him that this was too much. He continued by telling me that it was good for 24 hours and they had live music and amenities. I quickly told him that I only needed it for four or five hours for sleeping and that I would be out by 9 a.m. He said he did not rent rooms by the hour. I turned tail and departed. I knew the nearest commercial hotel or motel was in either Savannah, GA or in Beaufort, both a distance of some 50 miles. I chose Beaufort and got back into my auto, more tired than ever, because it was now about 4:30 a.m. In about an hour's time I was approaching Beaufort's city limits when a blue light police cruiser pulled me over. I jumped out of my car and held my arms skyward and said, "Please arrest me and take me to jail, I need sleep!" The patrolman looked puzzled. I then asked him what the infraction was and he stated that I had failed to put my auto lights on low beam which was required by city laws. I once again told him that the two of us were probably the only two souls who knew this, but I still wanted to go to jail for sleep. He said that he had a better idea. He got on his police radio and located me a place to sleep. He totally forgot about the infraction for which he had stopped me. Fairly soon, he told me to fol- low him. In a few minutes we were in front of a residential home that must have been a hundred years old and looked every bit its age. There was a sign in the front yard that explained that it was a "tourist home." *Any port in a storm,* I thought to myself. The officer left and I rang the old-fashioned doorbell, and finally a very old lady dressed in a bathrobe and a nightcap answered my ring at the door. She said that she had a room. I told her that I only required three hours of sleep and would she awaken me at 8 a.m. She said that she would do so. From the looks of the place, I didn't bother to inquire as to her rates. I had a hard time staying in bed without falling out since the floor had sagged so much on one side that the slope was at least 6-8 inches. I fell asleep promptly, not wanting to think about my very long day and many events, which had lasted some 23 hours. I went down to check out about 8:45 a.m. and was presented with a hand-written bill for $5.00 which I gladly paid. This rate was much better than the other one that I had been quoted. A salesman must watch his expenses, especially if he's paying them him- self, as I was. I thought of the advice my smart friend Rhett Jackson had given me at the steel building, that I should not attempt that long drive to Hilton Head and that I should get some prompt sleep and travel tomorrow. At least, I was now near Hilton Head, even though I probably looked 10 years older. Sometimes, you can outwit yourself. I was lucky enough to collect half of the dealer's debt, but buying was not brought up. I motored on to Charleton.

Please excuse my departure from my good friend, Rhett! One of the highlights of our friendship was the annual event that took place in spring time when Rhett put on his great fishing trip at Santee Cooper Lake. He would assemble six or eight good friends, and we would meet at the lake for four wonderful days of relaxation and good fellowship. We fished, cooked fish stew and other good things, played dollar-limit poker and especially a card game called "Oh, Hell." It has to do with drawing the queen of spades, then you could not help but say, "Oh, Hell" because you knew you had to drop out of the huge pot or match it to stay in. No one ever won or lost much money nor were the fish disturbed too much. These trips were repeated for many years and are etched in all of our memories. Lifetime friendships were formed!

Rhett had long dreamed of having a first-class furniture store in Columbia where, he said, "That's where the people are." This became a reality, and I'm happy to say it had a lot of Heritage-Henredon furniture on display. It was successful for years until Mr. Rhodes of Atlanta felt he should own it. He made a great offer to Rhett, and Rhett let him have it. Rhett next opened up what he thought was a simpler business, retailing carpet. It made moderate success and he finally sold this.

Next came the real love of his life, opening and operating a bookstore. He and his wife Betty named the Columbia store The Happy Bookseller. It was an instant success, and they loved the business. As was Rhett's custom, with his great personality and public relations skills, he rose to the top in the industry. Of course, this was before Barnes and Noble mega-stores. He was elected president of the National Booksellers Organization. On one occasion, he went to the Oval Office to present Ronald Reagan with a best-selling book. Rhett had reached the Big Time once again — and he was still my dear friend.

What made our friendship so unique was that Rhett is decidedly liberal in his views and I am very much a conservative. Our views were exchanged with neither yielding or being converted. We had enough love and respect for each other that this difference never was an issue. Maybe it's true that opposites attract.

After an unsuccessful try at politics, Rhett was appointed to be the chairman of the South Carolina Parole Board. As liberal and compassionate as Rhett is, I figured he would empty the prisons. But he used some restraints, and the people reappointed him for several terms as chairman. For years before and after his parole board experience, he made it a practice to be at the exit doors at the state jail and hand each freed prisoner a dollar bill and his business card. Rhett was simply practicing his deep Christian faith. He let each prisoner know that someone believed in him or her and wanted to inspire them that there was another way other than crime. What a friend to have! My excellent and good friend Rhett Jackson continues to inspire me.

Rhett and Betty enjoy frequent trips to Alaska, sometimes in the winter, to visit son Jim and his wife Megan. Jim is now a lobbyist for giant utilities in Alaska and doing very well. Megan was originally a schoolteacher in Alaska and began training sled dogs. She participated in their famous race, the Iditarod. Betty and Rhett's daughter Kay lives in South Carolina and has a family that the Jacksons visit often and love so much. My wife Dixie and I visit with the Jacksons as often as possible, and they visit us mostly at our little summer cottage named Timbuktu at Gingercake in western North Carolina. Our friendship is as fresh as it was back in 1951 when we first met in Chicago. That is 51 years and growing. We send our love and best wishes to the Jacksons.

CHAPTER 9

A Few Other Friendships

A Dream to Sell

*I*t is always very dangerous to list names in writing a book as this. Invariably, you leave out names you should have included. But in a career as long as mine was, my brain cannot possibly remember all the outstanding people with whom I came in contact that meant so much to me and who helped me be a better person in the sales world. With this danger in mind, however, I will charge ahead and do my best. My apology to anyone omitted! I will cite these people in alphabetical order.

Charlie Blair: In 1958, when I met "Big Charlie Blair," he was a salesman for Schoonbeck in the greater Washington, DC; Maryland; Virginia and West Virginia area. He had earlier worked with Jack Campbell at Tomlinson Furniture in High Point as a fabric specialist. They were very good friends. Charlie, in his territory, set enormous sales records. When Schoonbeck grew larger after the merger with Henredon, he was elevated to vice president of sales for the Upholstery Division of the company. He was well suited and did an outstanding job. I do believe he could give the best sales meetings in the retail stores of any person I ever knew. He traveled nationwide and helped establish our line as the finest. I learned so very much from this gentleman!

Roy Bradner: As a very young and aspiring High Point native, Roy Bradner decided early on that he wanted to train at Tomlinson's of High Point to become an excellent factory superintendent that manufactured upholstered furniture. He studied hard and observed the best factory craftsmen in the country who worked at Tomlinson. He was very successful in his undertaking and was later named as their superintendent, the youngest in the industry. When his associates at Tomlinson, Jack Campbell and Charles Blair, moved over to run the NC Schoonbeck Company (later to merge with Henredon), they called Roy to come as well. Roy was a real whiz kid in the business. His keen abilities and product knowledge enhanced rapid growth of Henredon. He and his longtime friendships with Jack Campbell, president, and Charles Blair, sales manager, combined to rocket our upholstered division to amazing heights. It takes real talent and passion to ride a rocket into outer space! I salute Roy and this outstanding team. It is ironic that these three special friends of mine come together in alphabetical order.

Jack Campbell: I first met Jack through my mentor and fellow salesman at Heritage-Henredon. Steadson Williams had known Jack when they both were at Tomlinson. When Heritage-Henredon split in 1958, I recommended to Henry Wilson at Henredon that he should acquire Schoonbeck, all due to the fact that Jack Campbell was key to our future success. Negotiation soon began, and Jack helped Henry to persuade Ted Schoonbeck in Grand Rapids, MI to finally merge. After we came together, with a pre-merger upholstery volume of $3 million to $4 million annually, Jack, in short order, had us up to almost $40 million in no time. He was a people person, and everyone loved to work for him. If you had a problem, you would go in and talk to Jack about it. He was so positive and smooth that after 15 minutes you felt good and the problem disappeared. Later in the day, you would say to yourself, "What did he really say to me?" Jack Campbell had a very great influence on me and my sales career. He would help me do anything that I asked him to do. Not everyone in life can qualify in this regard!

Wes Collins: One Saturday morning in the late 50's or early 60's, Henry Wilson, Sr. called me at my home in High Point to tell me that he was in the process of helping Bernhardt Furniture Company of Lenoir, NC, get into the upholstery manufacturing business. He asked me if I knew of a young and capable man that could qualify for Bernhardt's new factory superintendent. My mind went to one person,

A Dream to Sell

Wes Collins of Jamestown, NC. Wes had been a Marine fighter pilot in the war and was very smart and a hard worker. He joined Heritage Furniture Company the same day I went to their factory as a trainee to become a salesman. Wes aspired to become an upholstery superintendent. We became great friends. Wes did go on to become the assistant superintendent of Heritage under the famous Earl Clark. I told Henry that Wes was the man for the job at Bernhardt. Henry also asked if I knew of a seasoned person who could help Bernhardt with the layout and design for their upholstery plant. I immediately thought of Earl Clark, who was in the process of leaving Heritage. Henry met both of these candidates, and in concert with Bernhardt, hired both men. Based on their outstanding performance, Flair of Bernhardt was born. An instant success, Flair continues to be a mainstay in the upholstery category today. Wes Collins later became president of Bernhardt, with a brief departure to Broyhill before returning to Bernhardt as president once again. His reputation secured, Wes was ultimately selected as president of the giant conglomerate, Universal International Furniture. It is truly a privilege to have helped launch such a long and prosperous career. Of course, Wes Collins, the Marine fighter pilot, knew how to fly before I ever met him. We all congratulate this very fine and successful gentleman!

Jim Connelly: Jim was the founder of Nite Furniture of Morganton — a born salesman. We had worked together for my Uncle Harry at Lazarus Clothing Store. He loved three things most in his life: wife Mabel, his retail furniture business and training and hunting bird dogs. At one time he was interested in cockfighting but found it was against the law. Everything that Jim did, he tried to do it well. He always put the customer first. For example, he knew that women were the primary buyers of furniture. He also knew that it took much time for women to make these expensive purchases. They would get nervous in doing so. Consequently, a female customer would need to go to

Chapter 9 – A Few Other Friendships

the bathroom pretty often. He had the cleanest, most up-to-date bath-rooms in the industry. He supplied them with everything a woman could possibly desire or have use of. It worked, and helped Jim and Nite Furniture Company to reach a great reputation and lofty sales. Jim Connelly was one-of-a-kind. Much to the surprise of all who attended his funeral and at his request, he wore a hunting suit, red hat and all, and at the cemetery, a bird dog was there and a hunter fired three shots over Jim's grave. We miss Jim! He taught me volumes.

Jean and Nan Davis: (Later Jean Davis Moburg and Nan Tomlinson Van Every) These two very talented interior designers grew up in Winston-Salem, NC and were accounts of mine for 30-some years. We still stay in touch. They were an inspiration to me on each and every call I made on them. I must tell you about Nan's lunches in North Wilkesboro, NC when she had her business there. She had a most famous cook who prepared the most delicious lunches for whoever was around at that time of day. Nan accused me of just driving around her town and waiting for lunch time before I made my call on her. Nan, you were entirely right! Two great friends even to this day.

Amos Estes: Amos was the manager and buyer of Whitley's Furniture of Zebulon, NC and also a son-in-law of the founder. Amos thought big and did big things. I met him in 1981 at the time I went to work for Henkel-Harris Furniture Company. His buying and ability made a believer out of me that I had not made a mistake in choosing Henkel-Harris. In the early years, his was my largest account. Death took Amos away much too early, but he left a great wife, Nancy, and two fine sons to carry on. Amos was special to me!

Albert "Ab" Fanjoy: When I first started to travel for Heritage-Henredon in 1951, one furniture road salesman instantly stood out to me as a real champion. He was "Ab" Fanjoy of the partnership of Fanjoy & Bowles of Statesville, NC. They had the United States Southeast for Drexel Furniture Company. Ab traveled North Carolina and South Carolina while Lewis "Lou" Bowles traveled Georgia and Florida. They were the highest paid salesmen in the industry. I decided that I would need to model my career after Mr. Fanjoy! I studied his every move, talked with him and finally, tried to emulate him. I had been at Duke with one of his sons, Weldon, so I knew the family pretty well. Ab was a dapper little Canadian who Henry Wilson, while president of Drexel, hired because of his experience as a salesman for Berkey & Gay (which was the first company that combined casegoods and upholstered furniture to form a complete package for the retail merchants — unfortunately they went broke in the financial crash of '29 and the crisis that followed in the early 30's). Ab amazed me in the quantity of product he sold his accounts. He would tell them, "You can't sell much from an empty wagon." He was the first to require his stores to have galleries of his product on their floors and back up the inventory in their warehouses. Ab was excellent in his ability to help the dealer select the right merchandise that sold quickly. As a result, the dealers did what he asked of them because he made them money. He possessed the courage of a lion. It didn't hurt that his Drexel line was "red hot." Well, I wanted to be a clone of Ab Fanjoy! In time, I would use all that I learned from this master salesman. I even smoked a pipe as he did. Henry Wilson did not think much of pipe smokers in that he thought them to be without zest. He told me one day that Ab Fanjoy and I were the only pipe smokers, in his judgement, that ever succeeded in selling. I took this as a huge compliment — just to be packaged with Ab Fanjoy. People need to have heroes to model their lives around — one of mine was Ab Fanjoy!

Ken Fuhrmann: Ken went to work at Henkel-Harris at a very early age for Mary and Carroll Henkel, the founders. Starting early, when the factory was small, Ken had to learn to wear many hats and was good with each hat and responsibility. He was the one who really knew what made the factory work. One of his expert areas was the buying of the lumber. He still does this as I write about him. This is no easy job and requires broad knowledge. He is officially the national sales manager and knows all of Henkel-Harris's customers. He has and still does work with these customers when needed. I remember wonderful meals that he prepared for the salesmen and customers, for he is a real gourmet cook. I always enjoyed his traveling with me during my eight wonderful years with Henkel-Harris Furniture!

Boyce Grindstaff: Forest City, NC is a rather small town which Boyce made into a mega-market for fine furniture. His winning, positive personality, attention to details, his wisdom and courage, his obtaining the best furniture brands in the industry and his selling these at reasonable prices, all made his family-owned furniture company into an empire. Boyce is the driving force with his family members and associates. He is always responsive to new and good ideas for improving his operation. Most years, he was the No. 1 salesperson and decorator in his store. How he has the time for all of this always was a mystery to me. I suppose it is his passion for growing his business. He always inspires me with his Christian ethics and his fairness. It was a joy to call on him. He always bought furniture very fast but properly. You had better be prepared as a salesman, because your time is short with him on a visit. I always had a long list of items ready for him to consider. As I have said earlier in this book, he is one of the best furniture buyers I experienced in my 44 years as a salesman. Boyce, along with others, was the driving force in my writing this book. He and his wonderful family remain to be good close friends.

Jack Greer: Jack and Joy Greer were close family friends of Betty and me, starting after college days. Jack was born on Beech Mountain, long before it became a famous resort. It was not the kind of place people bragged about as a birthplace. Jack's WWII service was, indeed, hair-raising! He was in the Italian theater and was captured by the Germans while searching for his best buddy during a nighttime pull-back of their outfit. He just knew he would find his buddy wounded and could deliver him back to his retreating company. Jack stepped on a land mine and was knocked out. He was captured the next morning and spent a year and a half in several of the German prisoner of war camps. Before he was liberated by the Americans, his weight had dropped to 75 pounds, and his body was in terrible shape. Jack survived and had a mild "hero's reception" back in Banner Elk, NC. I believe Jack had the most wit about him of almost anyone I've ever known — it was dry wit. I later helped him to enter the furniture industry, and he did very well until his untimely death in approximately 1985. He was a trusted friend in all respects. We had great fun playing tennis together. He dearly loved his family. I think that one of his greatest joys was when, annually, his boss, "Buz" Davis, president of Davis Cabinet of Nashville, TN, would allow Jack to use his golf membership at the Augusta Country Club and to invite three of his accounts to play for several days on that hallowed course.

The Dan Ham Family: This marvelous family of Prosperity, SC offered me many years of joy and success for four generations. Yes, I made the transition for four generations. It started with the great-great-grandfather Dan Ham. A perfect gentleman, he sometimes made it a practice of taking naps in the bank vault of a former bank building that he owned, connected to his furniture building. He had acquired the building after the bank closed. The reason for selecting this venue for his naps was because it was simply the coolest place in town. This was before air-conditioning. I often, in jest, accused him that he did so "just to be near his money." Next, I continued with Dan Ham II and his brother Walter. They continued the success begun by "Dad." Next came Dan III (Danny) and finally his son. This may be a record for one factory representative to accomplish. I think one of the greatest tributes I ever had came when my wife Betty died during a fall furniture market in High Point. My doorbell rang, and I opened the door to see the three generations of Hams that had come to express their heartfelt condolences. I was overcome. The Hams are deep friends who always cared.

Darrell Harris: I first met Darrell and his father in approximately 1975 when they came to the Henredon showroom in High Point to seek our line to sell in their very small store there in the city. Due to company policy at that time, not to open up any new accounts, I had to give them the bad news. They took the news graciously but said that there would be a time in the future we would want to sell to them. How true that was, as they now have one of the largest furniture operations in the world. Darrell taught me that one has to dream big dreams and have the passion to persevere. He has turned dreams into reality in a very big way. Congratulations, Darrell and family!

Larry Hendricks: I first met Larry while completing a call on Merrell Furniture in Mocksville, NC (incidentally, Larry's father and Bill Merrell were in business together much earlier) and looked across the street in a parking lot to see a man driving a very, very, old, maybe 1950, Mercedes. The driver, Larry Hendricks, approached me and asked me to sell him the Henredon line at his father's store there in Mocksville by the name of Hendricks Furniture. I told him it was not possible. Little did I know how persistent this guy was. A couple of weeks later, on a Sunday afternoon while my daughter Susan and I were riding our horses near Willow Creek Golf Course, we looked up and saw this Buick coming down the trail, running over small pine seedlings and rocks. On closer inspection, we discovered that it was Larry Hendricks. Someone at the farm where we kept our horses had told Larry approximately where we were. Larry got out of the car and approached us with more requests for the line. He talked for 20 minutes or more. Finally, Susan got my attention and said, "Dad, did we come to ride or talk about furniture?" This put Larry back in his Buick. We had many more conversations. Finally he told me he was leaving his father's business and wanted to buy a going furniture business that had some good lines. I thought of the Country Shop in Hickory, NC whose owner wanted to get out of the business after her husband had died. I helped Larry in his purchase of that firm which had most of the good lines. Larry was off to the races and has never slowed down to this day. As I related to you in an earlier chapter, Larry has the courage and heart of a lion! He dreams and buys big time. Two of his secrets: Do everything first-class, and don't be afraid to back up best sellers. He would review our national color page ads, and if he thought they were good, he would back up the items in the ad by buying them 12-deep. He "nailed down" his floor display of the contents in the ad, along with the ad poster itself. He never had to break the display because he had 11 more in the warehouse. That smacks of smarts and courage. Now Larry Hendricks is a giant in the furniture industry with 12 or more fine big stores in several states. He was and is still my friend.

Mary Henkel: I have already introduced this fine Virginia lady to you. She's the lady who gave me a job at Henkel-Harris Furniture Company and thus permitted me to go out of my long furniture career in grand style. After WWII, while her husband Carroll worked at U.S. Steel in Pittsburgh, they came home to Winchester, VA, Mary's home, for the Christmas holidays. En route, they had a serious auto wreck. This put both in the hospital. Mary's home was full of fine antiques, so during their recovery from the wreck, Carroll thought that he would like to see if he could reproduce a corner-cabinet Mary had. He did and on completion found out they couldn't get it out of the basement. The solution was to cut it in half at its waist and remove it from the basement. Mary loved to tell this story with the end remark, "That's when we decided to go into the furniture manu-facturing business and knew that we needed to know much more about the process of doing it." They went on and with much help from many, they built one of the great furniture manufacturers of fine furniture in the nation, all in solid cherry, mahogany, and walnut! Carroll did the manufacturing and much of the sales, while Mary did the designing and financials. They made a great combination of skills. Carroll came to an untimely death that left Mary with the task of doing everything. She had, by this time, some excellent people around her who made this possible. Mary Henkel, everyone's friend, rose to the top in her industry and was honored by her introduction into the National Hall of Fame by her peers. She invited me to sit next to her at this event. How honored I felt to be invited! We all loved the moment. I'm very sad to report that Mary died in November 2001, a passing of one of the great ones in our industry. God rest her soul! She will never be forgotten by me.

Stewart Hensley: Stewart succeeded "Uncle Frank" as president of Fowler Brothers of Knoxville. Stewart had been a naval officer on a destroyer in the South Pacific in WWII. His ship was sunk, but Stewart escaped by swimming away. He swam in the Pacific for several days until he was rescued. In so doing, he had injured his heart. He was returned to the west coast for recovery, and it was there that he met a pink lady in the hospital. They ultimately were married. Later, Stewart learned that she was one of the heirs of the famous Libby Owens Glass Company — money was not a problem on either side. They chose to go back to Knoxville to live, and Stewart took over Fowler Brothers. They seemed so happy. One day while in their store, Stewart invited me to lunch. We got into his beautiful, baby-blue Buick convertible and began to drive and drive. He said his wife, Marjorie, wanted us to come out to their farm and home built on a mountaintop with pastures in all directions. What a pleasure for me! When we finally reached their vast contemporary house that had been designed by Cliff Maye, one of the greatest contemporary architects of the West Coast, we were met by a gray-haired man who told Stewart that he would wash his car while we had lunch. Marjorie had a great healthy lunch for us, and when we finished she showed me around their beautiful home — including the movie theater for family use. On returning to Stewart's newly washed auto for the return to the city, I decided that to be wealthy, one would have to inherit it or work very long and hard, with the help of friends and lady luck, to arrive at Stewart's position. I also learned that one's place in the sun is not always forever. As it turned out, the Hensleys had a dismal end with much hard feelings. Marjorie moved away and Stewart died a premature death. Sometimes, counting your blessings is not enough. I discovered right then that money alone would not insure happiness, and I changed my goals from just making money to insuring a good and respected reputation of always doing honorable and noble things and let the money take care of itself.

The Jones Brothers of Smithfield, NC: Their names were "Punk," "Street" and "Smokie." They were characters, indeed. Their father worked in banking in the small town of Selma, NC. He taught them to "get out and work" if they wanted to amount to something. They did! Even through high school and college, they worked wherever they could make a buck. They even sold hail insurance to tobacco farmers at pretty good commissions. Finally, it was the retail furniture business that was their passion. Highway 301 ran through their area, and it carried thousands of "snow birds" who went south to Florida in winter. These snow birds had money, and they liked the prices the Jones brothers offered. Then, there was Raleigh nearby. In fact, all of eastern North Carolina was available to them. They profited by all of this and became one of the most dominant merchants in eastern North Carolina. They were street smart and intelligent. One of their keys to success was the fact that they divided up the vast responsibilities of running a very large furniture operation into three areas of control, with one brother responsible for each of these areas: Street had administration and finance; Punk, all inventories, warehousing and delivery;

and finally, Smokie, doing most of the buying. This was very smart in that all brothers didn't have to duplicate their supervision. If some problem came up in warehousing and delivery, Punk was asked to handle this problem for the other brothers. And, so on throughout the three divisions. It worked very well and allowed success. It was a real treat to call on these very different characters. They were all trips. They taught me to be very flexible, and if one of them knocked you down, get up as gracefully as possible and proceed as if you had not been decked. They did not mind speaking their minds on a variety of subjects. They were usually correct, and their tactics cleared the air for all of us who called on them. They made us money and at the same time accumulated a fortune for themselves.

Jack Krantz: Jack came from the great retail furniture store, Woodruff's of Charleston, WV, to be Henredon's showroom designer. He later was given a sales territory in West Virginia and Ohio. He disliked traveling, so he returned to High Point and designed many other showrooms in the industry and did some freelance interior designing. We were friends for over 40 years. Oddly, I was selected to conduct his funeral upon his death in 1997. This was an unusual honor for me in that I had never attempted anything of that sort before. Jack was a friend to many, in fact, at his funeral, I had never seen so many beautiful women, from 8 to 80. Jack was single. I think that Jack would have been pleased!

Hatcher, Bill and John Kincheloe: The Kincheloes operate a very fine furniture store in Rocky Mount, NC, — Bulluck's Furniture — founded by their grandfather. Hatcher Kincheloe and his family continued it with the addition of Wildwood Lamps. Hatcher was very conservative and rather pessimistic in outlook, but he was a very wonderful and classy man. He and his wife raised a great family, two of whom had key roles in the future of Bullucks Furniture. Bill succeeded Hatcher at the helm until he had the idea of venturing into the now-famous Wildwood Lamps and Accessories. This allowed John to take over the present Bullucks. I have a personal story to tell you: I knew that making and selling lamps and accessories was profitable. On a visit to Bill Kincheloe one time, I made Bill a proposition. Since they had experience in making local lamps, I proposed to put up all the funding for starting a national company to make and sell lamps and accessories for half-interest. I knew that they were very conservative with money. I also knew that they were a superb family, with high moral attributes. Bill seemed shocked at the proposition and said he would like to think about it. On my next visit several weeks later, I asked for his answer. He said that he had talked with the family and they chose to do the total operation by themselves. This was fair enough as I would be a silent partner with maybe limited sales contribution. Well, the rest is history. Wildwood Lamps and Accessories is world-famous, and they do an unbelievably professional job of presenting a world-class product. I congratulate the Kincheloe family on their success. I still say that I pushed them into success. They are still great friends of mine and a world-class family.

Bill and Buck Kester: These are the great merchants and people who took over from their father a family retail furniture business called Rose Furniture in High Point. I was unable to sell them Henredon due to our limited distribution policy, but when I took over sales with Henkel-Harris Furniture Company, they were dealers for that line. Rose Furniture was well on its way as a national furniture store. The brothers had built a large fabulous new store. They took me in and said they had a desire to grow with Henkel-Harris. I had the impression that they were a little skeptical of my reputation of volume sales. I slowed my pace and let them do it their way. After about a year they found out that I was their friend and only wanted to help them make money. I began to increase, slowly, my recommendations of quantities to buy and trained their sales force to sell my product. Results soared, and we made

Chapter 9 – A Few Other Friendships

beautiful music together. They finally discovered that "you cannot sell from an empty wagon." Since our deliveries were very long, I convinced them that they had to buy into future cutting and sell against these purchases. This was the same strategy that I was using with other big stores, and it worked. Since I retired in 1990, their business has gone to pinnacles unimaginable. I have a soft place in my heart for these two marvelous merchants. I hope it's the same for them as to me!

Carlton Mallory: What a guy! He not only helped me get my job with Henkel-Harris Furniture, but helped me prosper. We are still great friends today. Carlton graduated from Virginia Military Institute located in Lexington, VA. He loved the military, and after his active duty in the army he rose to the rank of colonel in the reserves. He is one smart individual and very much a student of the Civil War, naturally, since that great southern General, Stonewall Jackson, was himself a VMI instructor. After Carlton's military career was over, he went into the banking business. There he learned finance. Mary Henkel wooed him away from the bank, and he became officially vice president of sales for her. He was much more than this as he really had to run her company on a daily basis. They had conflicts, naturally, but he had great patience until he later was made general manager of the company by Mary's son, Bill. Bill had inherited the stock at a very young age from his father. One day Bill announced to his mother that he was taking over the company, but that he wanted Carlton Mallory to be vice president and general manager. Mary hit the ceiling but was helpless to do anything about it. Father Carroll had left the business to Bill, and Mary received the property which included the factory buildings. Carlton has made Henkel-Harris into a fabulous big company that now produces the premiere lines in the country. Hats off to a great Virginian, Carlton Mallory. He is my friend!

John Maness: John was the owner of the Serta Mattress franchise for many states, and his home office was in Greensboro, NC. I never worked for him, but opened many accounts for him from many of my own accounts. He always invited Betty and me to go on the Serta Annual Reward Trips that took us around the world. John was born in Leaksville-Spray, NC (now Eden) and was a nephew of Mr. Glass of Greensboro. He graduated from UNC-Chapel Hill and, as expected, was a very loyal fan. After college he went to work for his uncle at Dixie Bedding Company (now Serta) and later acquired the ownership of the Serta franchise. He married a High Point girl, Carolyn Jones, who is as lovely as she is beautiful. John kept acquiring other Serta franchises in South Carolina, Georgia, Wisconsin and Nebraska. It is quite an operation. Everyone, I mean everyone, simply loved to work for him and do business with him. His was one of the first companies in the country which had award trips to foreign countries. This contributed to the huge success for his business. His winners loved to say they were "taking a mattress trip" to wherever it was that year. The success was that they all became like family and no management families and key salespeople dared miss a single trip. The sales poured in. John and Carolyn put much planning into these fabulous trips, even going the year before to check out the premier hotels and the entertainment covered on the trip. They made improvements so that when we joined them a year later, all was perfect. Even though John is laid back in personality, he is a perfectionist. My friend John later retired and sold his business to key employees, and Dale Whitfield took over as president and CEO with Hamp Culler vice president for sales. The new owners continued the business without missing a beat. They later sold the company to another Serta franchisee who continues the great company and that great family tradition. The company's trips (25, so far) with Serta & Friends have been highlights in foreign travel for our family, and it all started with our meeting John and Carolyn Maness, our dear friends. Not only traveling with them, we were traveling with many of our own furniture accounts. That's "double dipping" at its best!

Eddie Merrell: This very dapper and enthusiastic young man who managed the family retail furniture business, Merrill Furniture in Mocksville, NC, is one of the most responsive persons with whom I ever worked. He is an excellent student of the industry. He has had many most interesting jobs in which he excelled. He still checks in with me to date. He often quotes me from the lessons he learned. He now needs to put all of this together and make some real money.

Frank Morris: Very few people will remember this distinguished merchant who ran Morris-Early Furniture in Winston-Salem. They hit their heights in the 1920s and 30s, and actually dominated the fine furniture and decorating business in parts of three states – the Carolinas and Virginia. The reason for their brilliant success was traceable to their great sales staff. They simply had the best people — 12 well-trained and talented men and women. I recall this in order to explain what a great lesson I learned from "Mr. Frank" one day in my earliest years as a road man for Heritage-Henredon in 1951. One day, as I was about to depart the one-time great store, Mr. Frank called me to his office. He said that he had a confession as well as some advice to give me. "Plato, I want to confess to you why this store is no longer viable and how you can help others not make the same mistakes I made. We, at one time, had the best sales staff in the region, so good that we became complacent. We never added new and younger people. One day, many years later, we woke up and found that our business was terrible because our people and their clients had grown old and didn't need fine furnishings any more. Then it hit me, we had not kept up-to-date by bringing in younger staff, at intervals, with their age group of clients. I want you to warn your stores never to make this fatal error. Tell them, regardless of their success, to keep refining their staffs and hiring the young!" Well, I took Mr. Frank's advice and did this for the rest of my career. It was harder to sell this idea than it was to sell my product. Not many people do long-range planning. Those who listen do extremely well. A belated thank you to Frank Morris, God rest his soul!

W.W. Morrison and sons Graham and Glenn: What a colorful and interesting family! Mr. W.W. was one of my first clients. He ran the distinguished home furnishings store, Morrison and Neece in Greensboro, NC. He was smart, wiry and an innovative merchant. He had as his assistant, Boyd Barker. Among the many things that they did right was to bring the great Otto Zenki, from B. Altman's, New York, to Greensboro to work for them. Their semi-annual model rooms were the talk of the Southeast. Mr. W.W. had two sons, Graham and Glenn. They showed their uniqueness early as they worked for their father while still in high school. Their father had his hands full trying to bridle these two. One weekend, Graham and Glenn decided that they should go to the beach. Their father somehow got wind of this and tried to stop the trip. Early on Saturday morning he presented them with an order, to be filled promptly, for an installation of a linoleum floor for a kitchen. He gave them a very rough sketch of the area to be outfitted and the pattern number. He told the boys to take the whole roll out to the house and custom-fit it. The boys, after their father left, realized the beach trip was off. Then Glenn spoke up and said he had a plan that would expedite the installation so they could get away to the beach. His plan was to use the rough sketch dimensions and cut the linoleum before they left the store. This would save them a lot of time, and all they would have to do is place the pre-cut on the kitchen floor after putting the permanent glue down. A very good idea, they thought. The only problem was that there was an inch or so around the edge of the floor that wasn't covered. Glenn said to Graham, "Don't worry, I'll handle this with the client." Sure enough, before they could get away, the client came in to inspect the completed job. She called the void to their attention. Glenn quickly explained that she was observant and that this was a new kind of linoleum that expanded as you walked on it and that they had allowed for this. The client seemed puzzled but accepted their explanation. So the boys hastily departed and would soon be on their way to the beach knowing the store would have to replace the floor covering, but this would be another day. I could relate many more Morrison brothers stories, but most are too risqué to write in a book. Suffice it to say, the brothers went on to have colorful lives and Mr. W.W. was married maybe four times, the last being at age 88 while he was in the Presbyterian Home in High Point. This family afforded me with many fine orders and much to laugh about!

Bill Rowland and Joe Murphy: Two of the finest gentlemen you'll ever meet. They teamed up to run the distinguished home furnishing store, Bradford's Furniture of Nashville, TN. It was always a pleasure to call on them with the hope that just a little of their class would rub off on me. Their talents were complementary as Bill was the more conservative and with superb business abilities and Joe was the one who had the dash and buying abilities. I think that they both liked me as they honored me with great purchases. Rooms were hard to come by for the High Point Furniture Markets, so Betty and I made a downstairs apartment available to them, as our guests, for a number of years. Our families became very close friends. Our family spent several memorable Thanksgivings with them in Nashville, and on several occasions we invited them to our little cottage, "Timbuktu" at Gingercake, near Linville, NC. Our family has wonderful memories of all these occasions. So, I guess, you can mix business with pleasure!

Arthur Seelbinder: Yet another older gentleman, whom I met early in my young career, was a man most feared by salesmen, Mr. Arthur Seelbinder of Seelbinder's in Memphis. I had heard of his ill temper and great talent before I met him. He was German and an excellent interior designer with a vast following. In addition, his hobby was raising and showing a large collection of homing pigeons which he kept at a location behind his beautiful store on Union Avenue. There was a small circular drive in the front of the store that one could enter in the evenings to see two fabulously decorated rooms with live fireplaces in both rooms. They looked just like a living room that one had just left to get milk and cookies and return to read, sitting in your comfortable lounge chair. What a flair for reality and sales! A good, older friend of mine, Mr. Al Lark, who represented Karastan Rugs and Carpets, had told me how I should call on Arthur. He said, "First, he has an aversion to straw hats and will not buy from anyone who wears one." Arthur, himself, wore a French wool tam cocked to one side. Al said that I should buy a regular felt hat and, when I arrived at his office, before going in, I should toss the hat into his office. If it stayed, I was welcome to follow the hat into his office. If the hat came back into the hall, Arthur was too busy to see anyone. I did just this, and my hat stayed in and I finally got to meet Arthur Seelbinder. This procedure worked, and we developed a great friendship and did mutually profitable business which continued later on with his son, Oscar. I never did forget to ask Arthur how his pigeons were and he always took time out of his busy schedule for us to visit the prized homing pigeons.

In remembering a unique person and his pigeons reminds me of another story about a bird! It seems that two quite different people met in WWII. One was a very proper New Englander and the other a redneck from Texas. Later, the Texan had managed with luck to have oil discovered on his barren small ranch and had become very wealthy. He decided that he would turn his ranch into a model one by spending a lot of his found money. Once it was completed, he wanted to brag a bit so he invited his Yankee friend down to see his results. His Yankee friend turned him down several times, but finally made the trip south. The newly- rich Texan put his friend in a Jeep to drive him around the ranch. While driving, they encountered a bird which flew away as they approached. The Yankee friend said, "What kind of bird was that?" The Texan declared that it was a bird of paradise. The Yankee snapped back, "It sure is a long way from home!"

Harold, Milton, Ralph and Randy Short: What a distinguished and successful family that founded and operated Mecklenburg Furniture Shops in Charlotte! Harold had come up from Atlanta to work for J.B. Ivey Company in Charlotte. Later, he opened his own store there in Charlotte — Mecklenburg Furniture Shops, located on the outskirts of the city. He chose to grant a 20 percent discount in the new format. Consequently, I suppose, he was the first discounter in North Carolina. He was highly successful and a "born-again" merchant. He assembled a great staff. The time frame was approximately 1946. Son Milton went on to law school and practiced law before he entered politics and was elected to City Council in Charlotte. After college, Ralph joined his father as his assistant. If you wanted to be successful, you had to sell Mecklenburg Furniture Shops! I did so, and they made me look like a better salesman than I was. Their ads were of blue ribbon quality that sold home furnishings. On the surface, Harold was demanding and a taskmaster. Down deep, he was wonderful. The store had approximately 10 decorator-salesmen who were very effective. Mr. Harold told me he only hired people who could sell and that he could teach them how to decorate. He believed it was far harder, if at all possible, to train a person to sell. I learned he was 100 percent correct. Later, the company was able to move to a brand new building on Providence Road in the city. Their success soared. It was the kind of store that was a delight to call on and learn from. Ralph finally took over the store and continued the success. Milton later joined the operation. Randy, Ralph's son, finally had his hand at the tiller. All in all, Mecklenburg Furniture Shops was one of my favorite stores.

Emmett Stevens: Emmett's mother was a Broyhill from Lenoir, and maybe this led him into the retail furniture business. As a youngster,

A Dream to Sell

Emmett excelled in football and was a legend as a Lenoir High School quarterback. When I met Emmett, he and his brother Bob were operating Stevens Furniture of Lenoir. They moved a lot of furniture for me, and we were very good friends. Emmett loved golf and played on many days. Many road salesmen told me that playing golf with their store owners was the way they sold them furniture. I never subscribed to this theory. I did, however, write a big order once on the golf course, and it was from Emmett. The story goes like this: I had an appointment with Emmett to try to sell him a red-hot upholstery special, but I arrived too late to present it to him before he left for the golf course. I had only missed him by a matter of minutes. So, I jumped into my auto and hightailed it for the Cedar Rock Country Club. There I found Emmett limbering up on the first tee with his foursome. I dashed over to him and quickly explained the furniture deal. His partners seemed a bit dismayed. What I was trying to do was find a time, after golf, to work with him. Much to my surprise, Emmett said, "If this is such a good deal and you're in such a hurry, why don't you go to your motel room and write me up about $35,000 worth of it." I was teased for years for my persistence. Whatever works for you, do it!

Maurice Talley: This very close friend had a great influence on my personal life as well as helping me immensely with my business career. Maurice had great furniture making knowledge, but more importantly, he was a person you just liked to be around. He was born a Moravian, in Winston-Salem, and that religion demanded that its followers be educated in double majors — one with which to make a living and the other to entertain yourself and others. Maurice selected furniture making and the clarinet. He learned well! He was so good at the clarinet that he joined a big band and toured the country, but later decided he should get a real job. He rapidly rose in the furniture industry. His personality and know-how attracted the attention of Henredon Furniture. Craftsmen took to him for advice and his personal skills. A natural love affair was established quickly and lasted for the rest of Maurice's long life. He knew how to manufacture very fine furniture and did, always. He understood all of the old ways of making furniture that proved themselves year after year, but he also adapted to the new technology that came along. He probably knew more about woods than anyone I have ever known. He was Henredon's vice president for manufacturing until he retired. His family visited our mountain cottage often. Talley loved to get up early and cook our breakfast on an open grill by a mountain stream that flowed through our yard — Upper Creek. I can taste that wonderful food, even today. He and his family loved Gingercake so much that they bought a beautiful home with a view located there. He entertained us often with his clarinet and his many funny stories. What a class act Talley was — not many of them are around.

Gene and Sam Taylor: Their father was a no-nonsense, hard-nosed businessman who founded Taylor Furniture Company in Johnson City, TN. I was scared to death of him, as were his two sons, Gene and Sam. He was smart, however, and very successful. Gene, the older son, was educated to be a preacher but later turned his collar around and joined the furniture company. Sam studied at the University of Tennessee and joined the company also. Their father did not drink whisky and he forbade his family, as well. The sons felt otherwise. They slipped around and had a snort or two. Since Johnson City was in a "dry" county, they had a hard time obtaining whisky. The boys instructed us traveling men to bring North Carolina whisky over to them on our calls. It was necessary if we wanted to secure an order. One Halloween afternoon, after their father had died, Sam and the salesmen in the store started drinking, and he announced that they were going to have great fun that evening. Sam was also a politician and had managed Estes Kefauver's Tennessee campaign when that senator ran for president. Sam actually was elected to the

A Dream to Sell

Johnson City City Council. Back to the Halloween night story. Sam took his semi-drunk salespersons out to a suburban fire station in town and proceeded to have the firehouse people tell them all about how to operate the truck and how they used it. Sam's being on the City Council was the key. Then Sam told the firemen that he and his "volunteers" wanted them to take the night off, since they had such long hours, and that he and his boys would man the station. As the regular firemen reluctantly left, Sam mounted the fire truck to drive it out of the station. He told his salesmen to swing on, and they began to drive through a very fine neighborhood — all the time ringing the bell and giving small blasts on the siren. Cars fell in behind them as they slowly moved through the neighborhood. After ten minutes of trying to figure out what was going on, the policemen finally came alongside the fire truck and found that no real firemen were aboard. He arrested the whole bunch and took them to jail. This quickly sobered up the crew. Sam telephoned his brother, Gene, to come down to the jail and get him out before he was booked by the police. Gene didn't know what to do, but on his way downtown, the solution came to him. At the police station, he whispered to the police desk clerk that his brother Sam had terminal cancer and the family was having much trouble with him. Gene assured the police officer that Sam was a city councilman and if he would release his brother, they would try to comfort him. The policeman did so and the brothers left the jail. The rest of their salesmen remained. The brothers would deal with their release the next day. The Taylor brothers were real characters, but we all had good business from them. The stories about their escapades would fill volumes.

Steadson Williams: Steadson Williams worked for many fine furniture manufacturers before he joined Tomlinson's of High Point, where he was one of the top salesmen. He later moved over to Heritage-Henredon several years before I joined them. He was excellent in many ways with the exception of his hard drinking problem. Henry Wilson, of Henredon, was looking for a furniture designer and asked Steadson if he knew of a good one. Steadson quickly suggested a friend by the name of Ben Jones who lived in Florida. Henry asked, "Isn't he gay?" Steadson fired back, "For God's sake, Henry, you aren't hiring him for breeding purposes, you are hiring him to design!" That was Steadson at his best. Since I did not drink, Henry Wilson asked me to room with Steadson at the Chicago markets in the winter and summer, and possibly Steadson would slow down his drinking during these critical market times. I did, and I believe it helped. But I was the biggest winner in this arrangement. We became close friends, and it was Steadson who taught me the fine art of maximizing my sales. He was a master of the trade, and I absorbed his great lessons. If I have had any success in my career, much of it should be credited to my friend "Steady." It is hard to put into writing what I learned from this master over 20 years of lessons. To list briefly the essence of this learning, I would make the following points: Never have to beg for an order; think big and lead your buyer upward; be respected by your buyers; appreciate the circumstances around your buyers; follow through on promises made; fight for your accounts with the management of your company; fight for key displays in dealers' showrooms; be a true friend, but never too close that your buyer can say no at critical and necessary times; keep your clients solvent — you cannot sell to a bankrupt company; truly help your accounts make money as a result of good advice; get into your customer's mind and find out "where he is." This is a fraction of what I learned from "the master." The good news about Steady was that he met and fell in love with a marvelous and beautiful German lady whom he married, as a second wife. It was she, with no nagging and threats, who motivated him to stop drinking. Yet another way to cure an alcoholic! The Lord knows that we can use all the methods we come upon. Steadson loved the mountains of western

North Carolina and with his lovely Dorothea, visited us often at Gingercake. Both are dead now, but their legacies remain. Steady was my dear friend!

In addition to Steadson being my mentor and dear friend, he was a very colorful person to be around. His experiences and stories would fill a book. I loved to go with him to landmarks in Chicago and have him tell me how Chicago was in the 20's and 30's when he attended the furniture markets there. It was during the Prohibition when Al Capone ruled the city. Steadson would take me to Gibbies, Capone's favorite bar where they featured Jimmy and Tommy Dorsey's band nightly. He also showed me where the St. Valentine's Day Massacre took place and the machine gun bullet holes in the marble front buildings that stood then, and even now. Steadson had lived three lifetimes and had done it all!

Randall Tysinger: That courageous, smart and innovative young man from Thomasville, NC took over his father's store, Tysinger's Furniture, when his father and mother retired. He was representing most of the national famous brands in that very small store, but could not, on demands from these firms, stock galleries of their furniture. He stalled them off to give himself time to switch to imported antiques from England and France. He brought it off in grand style, much to the surprise of all. Not many I know could have had the wisdom and courage to do this. He has been very successful and is well respected in the fine antique business. Buyers from all over the U.S., visiting the High Point furniture markets, routinely call on Randall to make purchases. Another proof that if you are flexible and innovative, you can succeed. My hat is off to a dear friend who always uses his head for more than a hatrack. Go, Randall!

Bess Weekly: I met and was privileged to know Bess at Mecklenburg Furniture Shops in Charlotte as she was fast becoming their No. 1 sales decorator in 1951. She had lost her dear husband to a heart attack. Bess was left to support a son and a daughter. She had worked in a paint store in Charlotte and was an expert with colors. Mr. Harold Short heard about her abilities and that she was a great salesperson with a big following, so he hired her. He would help her to learn the home furnishings business. She took a correspondence course from the New York Interior Design School to learn the fine points of the profession. This required her to go to New York for two weeks to take the final exam. Of course, Mr. Short paid for this. It was not long before Bess proved to be the store's best producer. One day I asked Bess what motivated her. She replied, "When I was hard pressed to raise two children and myself, I had to buy my clothes from Belk's bargain basement. That was my original motivation. When the children were educated and out on their own, I set a new goal for my life. I dreamed of having clothes with the Montaldo's label. I wanted that very much, thus I pushed very hard to accomplish this goal." She did this and much more. Finally, it was a fine reputation that she desired that took over her motivation. This is a real live example of setting goals to succeed. She was a marvelous story for me to include in my motivational training sessions to others who wanted to succeed. People can be motivated for a couple of weeks by hearing a dynamic speech, but for lasting effects, one has to have a driving desire for something they really want that will require them to work hard to accomplish. I thank Bess Weekly for teaching me this great lesson!

I want to salute all the salespeople in all of my accounts, along with their warehouse and delivery personnel who helped me be better than I would have been without their patience and help. Another salute goes to all the factory craftsmen who produced the great products that I had the pleasure to sell for them. And a final salute to all the many fellow sales reps who were competitors but dear and respected friends. They were mentors as well. All of the saluted people above were a great portion of my career. Thanks to all! One person, regardless of how professional he or she is, cannot do much without the help of an army of supporters!

CHAPTER 10

About My Wonderful
and
Special Family

During my attempt to write this book, I have applauded the many who helped me make my life and career possible. I have intentionally not dwelled on the most important people in my life, my wonderful and dear family. For without them, their love and understanding, I could not have followed a life of a traveling salesman. They always supported me and cheered me on. They had a horse in the race! After all, I was doing it for them as well as for myself. I always was there for them on all special occasions — birthdays, recitals, special events, big sports games and most of all, the weekends filled with hiking, horseback riding, camping and all the things they were into. All of us took nice vacation trips together. Some were to Florida, and there were cruises and two overseas vacations. We went to London once for Christmas. Another of the long trips overseas, we went for a three-week trip up the Nile River in Egypt and then over to Istanbul, Turkey. We had so much fun and laughed a lot together. Also, every six weeks, in my travel plans, I was in our local area and commuted home nightly. Altogether, we were with each other more than one might imagine. Now, I take great pleasure in introducing them to you.

I met the lovely and smart Betty Cashion in 1947 while she was in training to be a laboratory technician at Grace Hospital in Morganton, my hometown. Her boss was the most wonderful Dr. John Reece. Our courtship, at times, was a long-distance affair with many letters and a lot of hitchhiking, since I was in school at Duke University. After a while, evidently, she didn't think I was serious and announced that she had a job offer in Chile, South America. As it turned out, I was able to talk her into waiting until I graduated from Duke, which was in 1950. I'm sure glad that one of my first real sales pitches was successful!

Chapter 10 – About My Wonderful and Special Family

Betty Cashion was born in Charlotte on August 5, 1923. Her parents soon separated, and as a result, she was reared by her paternal grandparents in Charlotte. This was not all bad since it was a very large family in which her grandfather and two of his brothers worked for the Southern Railroad as locomotive engineers. They were happy-go-lucky people. The grandfather's income was sufficient and especially so during the 1930s depression when many unfortunate people didn't even have jobs. Betty attended school first in Charlotte, and later the family moved to the country, outside Charlotte, so she finished school there. She graduated from high school in 1941, just before the U.S. entered WWII. She was able to get a good job as an executive secretary with a big insurance company in Charlotte. Prior to this, however, she had the excitement of being runner-up in the Miss Charlotte beauty pageant. I only found out this fact long after I married her. She finally realized that being a secretary was not the career for her.

Her mother was the business manager of the Crossnore Orphanage in Crossnore, located in the mountains of Western North Carolina. Together, they decided that Betty should at least obtain a two-year college education. They decided that Lees-McRae College in Banner Elk was the place she should attend. Betty's funds were meager, so she had to work part-time to pay the expenses. One of those jobs was waiting on tables during the school year and at the Pinnacle Inn, a summer hotel sponsored by Lees-McRae College. Her major was medical secretary and also preparations for becoming a laboratory technician. This required much chemistry in which she excelled, and she ended up tutoring other students for a little extra cash.

After graduating from Lees-McRae College she went into further training at Grace Hospital in Morganton where I met her. We were married on Easter weekend, 1951, and honeymooned in Florida. Betty kidded me at the time that the real reason I married her was because she owned the two front tires on my auto while I owned the back two.

Thus, she said, we actually merged. We both knew this was a joke because we loved each other dearly.

We were childless for the first seven years of our marriage. During this time, she ran blood laboratories for a doctors' practice in High Point and later was a medical secretary for the High Point Hospital while I traveled my new 3-state territory for Heritage-Henredon Furniture Company.

Before we owned a permanent home in High Point, we showed dash by building a summer home at Gingercake. We entertained our many young friends there on weekends, and three couples among these guests actually got married later. There is something special about that place!

At the urging of Betty's medical doctor and our minister, we decided that we should try to adopt a child or two. Adopting from the Children's Home in Greensboro is a rather slow process. After 18 months they decided that they had found just the right baby boy for us. We named him Craig Albert Wilson, and he was a joy! Betty had decided she should quit work when the baby came, so she became a full-time mom. After another sixteen months, we were advised by the Children's Home that they had a little girl for us. Now our family was just right! We named the baby girl Susan Elizabeth Wilson. Joy reigned in the Wilson household!

Betty was a great mother and also was able to keep the house going. Because of the two children, we had to build a new house as our old home located at 609 Hillcrest Drive was much too small for the expanded family. We moved into our new home at 908 Parkwood Circle in the spring of 1963. Betty and the children spent every summer at Gingercake while I traveled there for each weekend. We were all very active in the First United Methodist Church. Betty was inducted into the High Point Chapter of the Junior League and was very active in the "Parson's Table" at our church.

Chapter 10 – About My Wonderful and Special Family

She loved to travel extensively in the U.S. via six-week bus tours. She took three of these. On one trip, she would take Craig and the other, Susan. Her last one was alone. She loved these trips and saw our entire country. Together, she and I traveled to more than 50 foreign countries around the world. Very sadly, in her 65th year she suffered a serious stroke and never recovered. This was on October 22, 1988. We had had 38 wonderful and happy years together. Sadness filled our home.

Let me introduce you to our older child — Craig Albert Wilson. As related earlier, we adopted him from the Children's Home Society in Greensboro. He was born July 5, 1959 (no wonder he was a fire-cracker!), and we finally received him four weeks later. Craig was full of life from the very beginning and never slowed down in his life. He was truly a showman. We had the right boy. He was educated in High Point schools, spent a summer at Hargrave Military School, and came back to Westchester Academy in High Point and graduated at High Point Central High School.

I must tell you a story about this special child: Craig wasn't the greatest person to work at manual jobs. He would rather work in public odd jobs and play the piano. I was into more sweaty chores and loved to mow our lawns. One Saturday morning, I was out doing my favorite thing, mowing, when it dawned on me that I wasn't being a good father in allowing our 12-year-old son to sleep so late on Saturday morning. I thought that I should be teaching him how to work. So I cut the lawn mower off and dashed to his room, threw open his bed-room door, pushed back his draperies and said to him, "Craig, what do you think Abraham Lincoln was doing at your age?" Rubbing his eyes and sitting up in his bed, he replied, "Dad, I don't know just exactly what Abe Lincoln was doing at my age, but I do know what he was doing at your age, he was President of America!" Ouch! He had got-ten me. I closed the drapes, shut his door quietly and went back to my mowing. Maybe that boy would make it with his mind rather than his back doing manual labor.

Craig attained an Eagle Scout award and also a "God and Country." He went on to graduate from Duke University with a degree in business. He then attended N.C. State University for more accounting and finally went to the University of Alabama Law School to receive a degree in tax law. He passed his CPA exam and took his first job with Peet Marwick in Atlanta, a Big Eight accounting firm, and later moved to Arthur Anderson, also in Atlanta. He was doing great with that career. We were so proud of him. His personality was wonderful, for he never met a stranger. He was a joy to have as a son and brother to Susan!

Now for the very sad part. Craig had lung problems most of his life, even though he was 6-feet-1 and looked the picture of health. He went into Emory Hospital to have a biopsy taken from his lungs with the new method of using a needle rather than cutting through the rib cage. It was an outpatient operation. He went in the hospital at 3 p.m. and was to be home by 5 p.m. Actually, they hit an artery with the needle, and he was bleeding badly. He was rushed into regular surgery, and they repaired the artery and gave him a blood transfusion. They put him into a critical care room, but by midnight, Craig died. What a shock when my daughter, Susan, called me about 12:30 a.m. and told me Craig had died. I could not believe it. He was 29 years old. He had died on February 3, 1989, just a day or two more than three months after his dear mother had died.

Susan and I were totally devastated. Half of our family was gone in just three months' time. It occurred to me, at that sad time, that my heretofore charmed life had taken leave of me. With many wonderful friends and our Christian faith, Susan and I regained our footing and started on that long trail of healing. Sadness, once again, had come to our home. Two very wonderful and important people in our small family would not be here anymore for us to love and respect on a daily basis. They are missed, but the many happy memories of them will be with us forever.

It is a real joy to get a chance to introduce you to our other child, Susan Elizabeth Wilson. She came to us by way of the wonderful services of the Children's Home Society of Greensboro, as did our son. Susan was born on May 26, 1962, and we actually received her on son Craig's birthday, July 5, 1962. What a birthday present for Craig to have a brand new baby sister. With our expanding family, Betty and I had already had plans and had begun construction on a new and bigger home on Parkwood Circle in High Point. We sold our little home on Hillcrest Drive and had rented a small apartment, mostly to store our furniture as we planned, as usual, to move up to our summer cottage and stay as long as we could stand the cold weather there. Susan arrived in early July and was a joy from the beginning. As an early fall arrived and our cottage was without central heat, we had a problem! We purchased a ton of coal to mix with the wood logs in the big fireplace. This gave us more heat and made the wood burn more slowly. However, the early winter winds caused down-drafts in the chimney, and smoke would come into the house. Our water pipes froze on many days, so we used the water sparingly. Susan slept a lot, and one day Betty took a close look and saw that she had a blue color. Being a rather new mother, Betty knew the medical problem called "blue babies," caused by a blood condition in children. She rushed Susan to a baby doctor friend of ours, Dr. William Patton in Morganton. After a short examination, Dr. Patton said, "Betty, you are not giving this child enough baths. There seems to be coal smoke on her." Betty was so relieved and confessed the use of a coal/wood fire and that our water supply was short for baths. About this same time, I was traveling in eastern North Carolina and I was, in fact, in a toasty nice motel in Rocky Mount. The weather was so cold! I happened to think that maybe Betty's car did not have enough anti-freeze in it to withstand this severe cold. So I called her at the mountain cottage to ask if she had checked her car's antifreeze. She was near the end of her rope by now and she replied, "If I had any antifreeze, I would drink it myself!" I knew, at that moment, that we had better move from that mountain cottage back to High Point for the rest of the winter. And we did promptly. We moved into that tiny apartment until our new home was ready in May. To all of our delight, we moved into the new home on Susan's first birthday, May 26, 1963. Smiles and joy came with this long awaited move.

Susan began her education at Northwood School and then at Griffin Junior High. Then she switched to Immaculate Heart of Mary Catholic School in High Point and finally to Central High where she graduated in 1981. She had always been attracted to the out-of-doors and sports. She had ridden horses since she was 2, first in front of my saddle and soon on her own horse. In high school she played varsity basketball, tennis, and soccer. She loved it. For summers, she attended Yonahlossee Girls Camp located near Blowing Rock. She later went there for three more summers as a counselor. She became better in horsemanship and learned rock rapelling. She later learned to ski and snowboard. If it was dangerous, Susan loved it! During high school, she enjoyed a six-week trip to Europe. She was becoming a young lady of the world. She was ready for college. She went to St. Mary's College in Raleigh for her first two years and then transferred, for her last two, to Elon College where she received a double major in child psychology and human services.

For her graduation, I asked her what she most wanted as a present. She replied, "What I really want, Dad, costs too much!" I asked her what that might be. She replied once again "I really want a three-month tour at the Outward Bound Camp located in Maine." Her mother hit the ceiling in protest. Since Susan was a beautiful young lady and had made her debut in High Point earlier, Betty thought that it was time for her to pursue more ladylike endeavors. Susan, however, prevailed and off to Rockland, Maine, she went. She was obtaining higher education in dangerous pleasures.

Her first job was near Atlanta, near her brother, as an outdoor counselor to troubled young girls at a school named Annewakee. In an effort to meet new friends as well as finding another dangerous sport, she joined the Greater Atlanta Kayak Club where she later met and married Wayne Gentry, their instructor. He taught her well, and she later became two-time world champion in the small-trick boat called a "squirt boat" and came in third in the world championship in the regular kayak. She was the chairperson for organizing and hosting one U.S. World Kayak event.

Susan and Wayne were married in June 1988, at our church in High Point, after having being talked out of having it at a lovely spot they had discovered on one of their kayaking trips down the Colorado River, at a waterfall in the bottom of the Grand Canyon! The wedding was nice, and we finally saw our beautiful daughter dressed as a bride and looking like a model. It was a most happy occasion for our family. Little did we know that this was the last hurrah for our family. In four months her beloved mother would die and three months later, her brother would also die. Now, it became my responsibility to be for her, mother, brother and father. Much more than I was prepared or qualified to do. I would do my best. I helped Susan and Wayne find and purchase a little home near Atlanta. We secured furnishings for it, and all seemed as well as could be expected. However, I'm sure she missed the advice and counseling of her mother and brother. The marriage which had begun so well ended in 1995. Susan moved to Asheville and bought a home there, in order to follow her love for the out-of-doors and kayaking. She appears to be happy and has added to her activities that of training search and rescue dogs. At 40, she has matured into the independent, loving and compassionate person that she has been developing all of her life.

From the time I first met Betty in 1947, and married her in 1951, through the rearing of our two lovely children, to date, has covered 59 years. We enjoyed many highs and a few lows. Mostly, it has been a time of joy. I, personally, feel blessed to have been surrounded by my family's support and love. Next to God, family comes in a very close second.

Soon after I retired at age 64, I was reacquainted with a Duke classmate, Norma Barringer of Durham. We were married in 1990. We never did really bond, so with a mutual understanding, we dissolved the marriage.

Because of this failure, I quickly busied myself in renovating and enlarging our little summer home at Gingercake. This was much fun and kept me very busy. I even put in central heat. I was planning on staying much more of my time in this little beloved home. After completing this labor of love, I found time to research the market for a person with whom I could spend the rest of my life and enjoy my retirement. With the help of friends, I was able to meet that person. This very nice and beautiful lady was Dixie Propst, a transplant to my hometown of Morganton. She is 11 years younger than I. We spent a lot of time together, hiking, canoeing, seeing many waterfalls in the vicinity of Gingercake and quite a few picnics. We both took our time looking each other over before we came to the point of that serious matter of marriage.

We both came to the conclusion that for better or worse, we should get married. We selected a quaint little stone Presbyterian Church near our summer cottage, located in Crossnore. We had a very small wedding on October 17, 1998 and invited family and a few close friends. We all dined after the wedding at Eseeola Lodge in Linville, which was nearby. Our honeymoon was in England for two weeks. Happiness, again, dwells in both of our lives. Love and charm has come back into my life and hopefully in Dixie's life as well. We intend that our marriage will last our lifetimes.

Speaking of family, I must say that I am blessed to have two very wonderful older sisters, Rosa Lee Jones and Marian McLean. Rosa Lee lives in Morganton, and Marian has just moved to Lake City, Fla. Throughout my life, we have always been supportive of each other and have had very special relationships to this day. There is nothing that each of us would not do for the other. They each have two sons. Rosa Lee Wilson Jones' two sons are Edwin who lives in Morganton and Richard who passed away in 2001. Marian Wilson McLean's two sons are Murphy who lives in Wellborn, FL and Thomas who resides in Birmingham, AL. We are thankful for them and enjoy them very much. We wish we could see them more than we do. My sisters are both widows now, and I love them very much.

A personal card to me from my mentor, T. Henry Wilson, Sr.

Mary Henkel, president of Henkel-Harris Furniture Company and Plato Wilson, 1982

Our long time friends [L-R] Rhett & Betty Jackson and Dixie Wilson, on a picnic along the Blue Ridge Parkway with Grandfather Mountain in the background, 1998.

Dixie and Plato Wilson at a Lees-McRae Scholarship Gala, Elk River Country Club, September 2002.

T. Henry Wilson, Sr.

Ralph Edwards

Donald Van Noppen, Sr.

Sterling Collett

FOUNDERS OF HENREDON FURNITURE CO.

"The Little Booger Band"
in concert at the Colonial Country Club, Thomasville, NC
[L-R] Mark Pierce, Bill Struss, Charles Bryan, Tom Gray,
Ray Wardell, Bob Hauser and Plato Wilson.

Our family:
[L-R] Craig, Plato,
Susan and Betty Wilson

"Timbuktu" in summer, at Gingercake.

"Timbuktu" Christmas at Gingercake, 1998.

Susan Wilson age 13, Lady and Rex, in front of Eseeola Lodge, Linville, NC after a day's ride over Grandfather Mountain, 1975.

[L-R] Susan Wilson and Elaine Travis riding Pepper and Lady, our horses, at Gingercake.

CHAPTER 11

Real Estate
and
Other Investments

A Dream to Sell

While I was learning the retail clothing business at age 10 in 1935, I also had a chance to observe my Uncle Harry Wilson and his real estate ventures. Much of this took place in the famous shoe department of Lazarus, then located on East Union Street in Morganton. This shoe department was the nerve center of Burke County, in that everyone came there to discuss what was going on in the county. My uncle was also considered a political boss of the county. Harry Wilson and his close friend, Harry Riddle, were 50/50 in all of their real estate ventures — Uncle Harry the master trader and Harry Riddle, who ran Morganton Savings and Loan, the "book man." It was exciting for me to observe these two at work, for they were complements to each other in talent. They were very successful, and all of this was not wasted on me. I dreamed that one day I would do the same, as a sideline.

My Uncle Harry had said one day that one should have a financial portfolio with a third in real estate, a third in stocks and bonds and a third in life insurance. This, he explained, was a hedge. If one or two of the investments went down, one for sure would be up. It would take some of the risk out of investing. Remember, we were just coming out of the great crash of 1929.

At this time, in 1935, the savings and loan banks needed people to put money in their banks so that they would have that money to lend. They lived on the "float." The Morganton Savings and Loan, operated by Harry Riddle, had printed up a little brochure entitled "The Richest Man in Babylon" with a theme of how to get out of debt and also how to stay out of debt. The answer was to pay yourself 10 percent first from your earnings. Surely you were worth 10 percent of what you earned! I was given one of these brochures by my uncle. At the time,

Chapter 11 – Real Estate and Other Investments

I was working for my uncle for $1.50 a week (after school and all day Saturday). So I started to save the 10 percent which amounted to 15 cents a week. I never stopped for the rest of my life.

My grandfather, John Wilson, had tried earlier to teach me business. He gave me a young piglet to raise and directions to keep books on expenses before I marketed the hog approximately a year later. I did as he instructed and tallied up the feed cost. I was unable to sell the hog for what I had invested. I went to tell my grandfather the bad news and he said, "Well, son, look at it this way, you had the use of the pig for a whole year." I then had learned that you don't always make money on business ventures. Later, my business expanded into leaf hauling to be composted and returned, being paid both ways; manure sales; milk and butter; share cropping; and later, during my college summers, working at Henredon. I had three jobs each week: in the factory five days; Saturdays unloading boxcars of cement for Morganton Hardware; and on Sundays, lifeguarding at Clearwater Beach, as I had my senior life-saving certificate. In my high school days, in the summers, I sometimes worked for Mr. Jim Harbinson, land surveyor. While out on surveys in the country, I would locate old buggies and surreys and buy them, usually for five dollars. I then refurbished and painted them and resold them for $50. I was doing okay and was saving a minimum of 10 percent — and most of the time one half!

My first year as a Heritage-Henredon Furniture salesman, I made $6,000 plus all expenses. I was married by then, but managed to keep my discipline of saving to a minimum of 10 percent of earnings that went into my investment funds. My first stock purchased was 100 shares of Jefferson Pilot Life Insurance Company.

While traveling for Heritage-Henredon, one day I was in the store of my dear friend, Rhett Jackson, in Columbia, SC. He told me that he had someone famous to introduce to me. It was Mike Mungo who had been featured in *Time* magazine as being a whiz kid in his real estate career. I had read about him in *Time* and was anxious to meet him. Rhett asked Mike to tell me his story. Mike was born in Lancaster, SC to poor cotton mill workers. At an early age, Mike's father died and Mike decided, somehow, he would get a college education by working his way through the process. He entered the University of South Carolina and held many odd jobs to pay for his education. Along the way, he took an interest in city planning, a profession in which there were many good jobs to be had. To gain more education, he taught city planning in graduate school where he learned a great deal more. Later he decided that his future was in real estate investments. He was very successful on his own, and at the same time very rich people brought him huge sums of money to invest for them with a 25 percent piece of each deal for Mike. In the process, he made too much money for his own good. He could not handle success. He started drinking and lost almost everything, including his health. Somehow he had later been able to make a comeback. The heart of Mike's theory was that as a city planner, he learned that by drawing a circle around the downtown prime property and then drawing continuous circles, at intervals, out of that area, one could find out where the best areas would be for real estate investments. This area would be on the main arteries out of the city and where one would find the decaying old residential homes. These old houses would soon be prime business locations when the houses were removed. He set out to try to buy homes on the corners and adjoining lots. He found out the northern portions of cities had the best chance for quality growth. Usually, the factories were located on the south side. He had the foolproof formula, and he was kind enough to share it with me. I finally asked Mike what motivated him in the beginning and he replied, "We buried our father on credit." I had learned two important lessons from Mike: (1) how to buy real estate property and (2) success can destroy you if you are not careful!

It wasn't long after meeting Mike Mungo that I heard "Tennessee"

Chapter 11 – Real Estate and Other Investments

Ernie Ford's story about why he stopped his nationally famous TV hour show in prime time. Ernie answered, "When I grew up very poor in Bristol, Tennessee, fire was the only luxury that we had. Fire warmed our little house; fire cooked our food; fire heated our water. Fire was wonderful. We also realized that if you got too close to fire, it would burn you!" Ernie continued to say that his whole life was his TV work and that as wonderful as the job was, it was destroying him. So, he just quit the job to save himself and his family. He had gotten too close to the fire. My thoughts immediately flashed back to Mike Mungo and how he let his success destroy him. Moderation is a great word to be studied and mastered.

Our first real estate investment was a little home on Hillcrest Drive in High Point, NC. We bought it brand new in 1954 for $24,000 and enjoyed it until 1961 when we sold it for $29,500. We were making money on our first real estate investment.

While traveling to Spartanburg, SC I ran into a man with a plan who wanted to share it with me. He was in the process of buying his second old peach orchard. He explained to me why it was such a good investment and entirely legal in all respects. The old peach orchard's trees were so mature that their production had declined badly. Besides, their variety was not the one that was selling in the current market. The orchard land was excellent. With an appraisal, he was still able to put a fairly high price on the old trees, and he had begun to amortize this portion of the purchase. He then plowed up and destroyed all of the old trees and used the balance of the unused depreciation to write off some of his income taxes. He then replanted new trees, and now he had a very large evaluation to begin, once again, to amortize. He said that he had an IRS letter that this procedure was permissible. He said you could do the same with old rental houses. Now, I knew from Mungo how to buy and from my Spartanburg friend, I knew how to dispose of obsolete properties. With my Duke University accounting degree, I was able to connect the dots.

Back in High Point on weekends, I applied the Mungo principle and was able to buy, over time, some 25-30 old homes in what would be, in a few years, prime business property with new buildings built there. I was in the rental business for a while, and that is not pleasant. The houses were ultimately condemned and were razed by me. I had the land at quite a bargain. I took the unused depreciation from the old houses as a tax write-off and then sold the raw land to my children's trust. I was able to find tenants for buildings that we built on the trust's land. I had practiced generation-skipping. The cash flow went to the trust, and I did not have to pay income tax on that.

I took the plan to Greensboro and found a run-down dental office building at a bargain and bought it for the trust. We updated the building in every way. With the remodeled building, I was able to lease it fully. Much later, an investor approached me to buy this building, and we sold it to him at a handsome profit.

I found the old vacant Dillworth Post Office in Charlotte one night when I drove through that neighborhood as I was returning after dinner. It was boarded up and looked terrible. I inquired the next day as to the cost. The building was a modern designed structure some 40 years old. It had 70 parking places with entrances on East Boulevard and also on South Boulevard. A great future location! I was able to buy the property for the children's trust at a small price, engaged a traditional architect and let the contract to renovate the building. We spent approximately $250,000 on the building's transition. This, too, was in the name of the children's trust. We rented this fine 10,000-square foot new building for approximately 15 years, earning more than enough to pay for it completely. We were advised by the City of Charlotte that it was classified as a historical site, so we were able from the beginning to take a handsome historical tax credit. At the time, the law stated that you could depreciate the life of the buildings in 15

Chapter 11 – Real Estate and Other Investments

years. We later made a gift of the property to a Charitable Remainder Trust, of which my daughter was the beneficiary. When the CRT sold the property at the very nice price, due to Dillworth's being prime property once again, no capital gains had to be paid since it was owned by a CRT. As a result of knowing Mungo, a Spartanburg friend and my Duke education, we were doing pretty good. Real estate is a good place to invest assets. Our thanks went to all who had helped us.

As one's income rises, one should think about investing in investment-grade municipal bonds since there is no federal or state tax due on their income, that is if you live in the state of the bond. I encountered another man of wisdom who told me how many of these municipal bonds to buy. He said, "Invest your age as it relates to your net worth." Example: If you were 75 years old, you would invest 75 percent of your portfolio in "munies." This is a hedge, as you get older, to protect against a stock market downturn. If one is younger, that person would have more time to recover and ride out a downturn in the stock market. It sounded good to me, and consequently our family, for years, has done this. It sure cuts down on your federal and state income tax bills as well.

After being in the real estate investment business on the side for years, I decided I should go to night school and take the real estate broker's examination. At the time, one could go to a community college one night a week for six weeks to satisfy the educational portion. Most people fail the broker's license test two or three times before they pass. That appeared to be too drawn out, so I took a one-day crash course that claimed if you did, they assured you, you had a much better chance to pass the first test. I spent a very puzzling day in Winston-Salem with all of these "young dudes" with fresh minds. I seemed to be getting the review a little slower than the rest. I think the instructor, who had already said he had spent part of his life as an odds maker in Las Vegas, sensed that some of us were falling behind, and he said to the class,

A Dream to Sell

"The test is given in short time frames, and it will be mostly multiple choice answers. Go through the various parts quickly and answer all you can. You should leave the hard questions for last. Go back over the skipped questions and quickly try again to answer them. Before your time is up, go back and select the letter C answer for all blanks. We know C is correct most of the times. The odds will be with you!" I passed the test with flying colors, and you can bet I had more than a few C's marked. I was learning that the odds should be considered in almost all ventures. I had a college roommate who used to say, "I've been accused of many things, but never of being brilliant!" I've learned in my life that if you aren't brilliant, you sure better be street smart.

Later, when my sales career matured, due to hard work and experience, our financial condition also became much more secure. Mr. Henry Wilson told me that I should contact his friend at Marine-Midland Grace Bank (MMG), New York City, about getting into the oil drilling business in which Henry, a friend, Charles Robbins, and Mr. Robbins' mother were doing. MMG had a customer of the bank who used them for loans to drill development wells in Texas. Developmental wells are much safer to drill, in that one knows there is oil below, opposed to a wildcat well. The Texas driller was a Mr. K. K. Amini, and he took large percentages of ownership in each well drilled. So, if my idol Henry Wilson, was aboard, his financial advisor and his mother also in on this, I thought our family should join them. We would take anywhere from 2 to 5 percent in each well drilled. With depletion allowances and drilling expenses, we could write off, from our income taxes, some 90 percent of our payments and reap the cash flow from the wells drilled. The trouble was you had to continue drilling to overcome the cash flow. In essence, your investment looked like an inverted pyramid with the point at the bottom. The more invested, the wider the point grew each year you rolled over even more in new wells. In the 130 wells that we invested in, we only had four dry holes. I was told by many people that I would put more money into the ground than I ever would get out. The trick is knowing your driller and his honesty and track record. Of course, the write-offs reduced our income tax payments. Here again, my trusted and educated friends were helping our family. When we started drilling, we could make money at the $5-a-barrel price that we were receiving. During the Middle East crisis in 1972 - 75, oil prices soared to near $40 per barrel. What goes up usually comes down at some point. After the crisis was over, oil prices fell back to $6-$7 per barrel. That is when I decided to get a certified appraisal of all of my oil wells. It came in very low. I then sold my total interest to a newly formed limited partnership: SECA, Ltd. (Susan E. and Craig A.— our two children). This was generation-skipping. Susan and Craig Wilson had 1/2 percent interest each and were the general partners, while their C & S Trust (Craig and Susan) held 99 percent of the ownership of "SECA, Ltd." Son Craig was by now a CPA and held a tax law degree. He helped us set this framework into motion. He even placed a spendthrift clause in the trust that would not allow either child to pledge any of the assets if either went on a spending spree. We considered the oil ventures as a part of our real estate holdings. I had planned for Craig to take over all these ventures and manage them instead of me when I retired, but unfortunately he died at 29 years of age. It was a very great loss to our family in every way. This meant that the responsibility came back to me. I had certainly not planned for this to happen. At my age then, 65, I had lost a bit of the dash of my earlier years. In the earlier years my life ran on parallel tracks: "the selling game" and "the investment game." It was exciting, fun and most rewarding.

The reason I called my business life games is because I learned early in my career that business and sports are closely related: You get knocked down and you get up and continue; you get bad calls from the referee, but you keep playing; timing is everything; opportunity only lasts a split-second, and you must keep yourself morally strong and physically fit so you can complete the game and be successful. It is one of the best games in town. Winning is important, as are your family, faith and reputation. My endeavor was to score successfully in all of these categories.

CHAPTER 12

Foreign Travel

A Dream to Sell

One might think that a person such as I, who had traveled an average of 60,000 miles a year by auto and 5,000 miles by air would have enough of traveling. Especially, if that person had done this for 44 years. Some friends likened this type of business travel as similar to a "squirrel in a cage" kind of travel. Not me. I found all of this travel exciting, interesting, fun and challenging. I could not wait to be on the road. My 20 speeding violations should attest to my haste in getting to the next account to share the good news that I had for them.

I have been asked through the years if all the road noises surrounding hotels and motels that were often on busy highways or interstate roadways affected my sleeping abilities. My answer was no. One can tune-out all types of noises. Years ago, many people in towns and cities lived on or near railroads or had grandfather clocks that chimed all night long. They simply tuned the sounds out of their minds. In fact, I sometimes had trouble sleeping at home due to the quietness. I even gave thought to recording the rumbling sounds to be played while I slept at home. My family quickly negated this wild idea.

Like most working people, our family had planned to do our foreign traveling after we retired, when we had the time and funds to do so. This all abruptly changed when I was 44 years of age. I was called to the bedside of my life-long friend, Bob Small, who lived in Memphis. Bob advised me that his doctor had told him he had about one week to live. Bob was 45 years old. Shock and disbelief came over me. He went on to tell me that the surgeons had operated on him and found a brain tumor that could not be removed. The incision was closed, and he was given the bad news. Bob asked if it was possible for Betty and me to fly out to Memphis because he had something to tell us. Naturally, we caught the next flight with the pressing question on our minds: What does one say to a young and dear friend who has but one week to live? As you can imagine, on that long and sad flight, our minds worked overtime for the answer to that question.

But there is more to tell about this exceptional young man and friend from childhood as we grew up together in Morganton. Bob lived half a block from our house. Our fathers had grown up as close friends as well. Both of them had alcohol problems. Our only hope was to learn to be street smart. It was Bob who had the brilliant mind. He was a straight-A student in school. When WWII came along, Bob went in the Navy and I joined the Army. We were separated for the first time. I arrived home from the war first and enrolled at Duke University for a free G.I. Bill education. Much to my delight, here came Bob to Duke one semester later. I am sure that our mothers were responsible for our being in the same place. Bob was my tutor in several very tough cours-es. He was just another special friend along the way who threw me a rope just when I needed it most. We both graduated from Duke in 1950. Of course, Bob's grades looked a little better than mine.

Bob accepted a good job with Liberty Mutual Insurance Company and moved to Nashville. He later became head of the mid-continent for all adjustment claims and had 28 lawyers working for him, even though he was not a lawyer himself. At a bus stop in Nashville, Bob was attracted to a fellow rider whose name was Martha and who was most beautiful. They later married, and I visited them often as I trav-eled through their city. Later they moved to Memphis. Bob had always had an interest in Boy Scouts. As a scout growing up and later as an adult in Memphis, he was made Scoutmaster for the greater region. He brought large groups of scouts to hike the Linville Gorge area which gave us a chance to visit and hike together. That area is very close to our summer home. Martha, Bob, Betty and I took many summer vaca-tions together. We stayed in touch.

We arrived in Memphis for our last visit with Bob. Betty and I never did come up with the proper conversation to have with Bob. When we actually saw him, he was at his home at his request. On seeing us, he took over the conversation saying, "I know that you have wracked your brains as to what you should say to me when you arrived. You don't have to say a word because it is my time to talk with you and give you some good advice." What a turn of events! Bob continued, "You two have worked long days and saved and invested your money for all these years. You really have not enjoyed yourselves. For me, I do not have a lot of money, but I have the most wonderful family one could imagine. I own a Sears and Roebuck shotgun and hunt often. I spend much time with the young people in Boy Scouts. My home is almost paid for, and I am at peace with the world and ready to go to my maker."

Then he zeroed in on us. "I feel sorry for you two. You are postponing living. I want you to promise me that you will take two vacations a year, one as a family and the other as a couple. You have to promise this without fail. I will feel like I have accomplished much if I hear you give me your pledge on this last request of you." Betty and I looked at each other and then turned to Bob and said, "Bob, thank you for reminding us, in a dramatic way, of something that we will do for you and ourselves as well." At that moment, we received the best advice we could have had, and that started our thoughts in the direction of that long-postponed foreign travel that for years had been on the back burner. Bob died shortly and left his mark on Martha, Nancy and Bob Jr. What an individual! Friends are the present that you give to yourself. We had lost a dear friend, but his wonderful memory will last a lifetime.

This has been a very roundabout way of telling you of our joy of international travel. Shortly after the promise to Bob, Betty and I decided to take a second honeymoon. We went to Jamaica for 10 days. What a blast! We were hooked, if our play money held out. Bob had opened our lives to the great "out there." The year was 1968.

Since our marriage in 1951, Betty and I took trips to Florida to Pompano because that was one of the places we visited on our modest honeymoon. From 1951 to 59, before we were blessed with children, we spent 10 days there in the month of March. We watched that tiny village grow into a metropolitan city in those years. We did not like what happened to our village of Pompano. We also discovered that we could travel to foreign countries for the same money.

On one of those Pompano trips, we decided to ask my mother and father to accompany us, because neither of them had ever seen the ocean, visited Florida, or flown on an airplane. When I extended the invitation to them, stating the three "firsts" that they could have, my mother said, "We would love to go, but I think we should go through the country by auto." I said to her, "Mother, you must be afraid to fly? You are a Presbyterian by birth, and I'm sure you believe in predestination. You have always taught me that one had a lifetime that was predestined, so you should not worry about flying." She quickly announced, "I'm not worried about my clock running out, I'm worried about the pilot's clock running out." So we drove through the country. We all had a grand trip. The first thing my father did was go to a department store and buy himself a pair of walking shorts so he could stroll on the beach and be near the ocean that he and mother had never seen.

In my furniture travels, I discovered that mostly my smaller accounts spoke often about just returning from some exotic trip that they had just enjoyed. Their host was either General Electric or Serta Mattress Company. I thought to myself, *Here these little store owners, without overall means, are traveling all over the world and having the times of their lives. I was under the notion that only the "rich" traveled to these places.* I inquired more about these trips. I was told by Garland and Marjorie Hutchins of Hutchins Furniture in Kernersville, NC that they traveled free as a reward for selling so much product. I asked if it were possible for me to buy two trips and go with them. Garland informed me that if a store won two trips that they could purchase a matching two trips. I signed up for Betty and myself, immediately. We were off to London for a week. We discovered that most of the people on these trips were accounts that I called on and were dear friends. The next trip was to Copenhagen, Denmark. We had a very good thing going. We were beginning to be world travelers.

One of the bonuses of these trips was the chance to meet and become friends with the owner of a very large franchise for Serta Mattress Company, Mr. John Maness and his lovely wife, Carolyn. A nicer couple one could never meet. John is very low-keyed but down deep he is a perfectionist. These trips were planned to the hilt. Once the location was decided, they would take a trip to that destination, as a trial run a year ahead, to find out how it was and how it could be improved. They did their work well. All of their trips were fantastic. Their format was to select the finest hotel in the major city to be the base of operation. We would then take day trips out of there and return each night to the comfort of our hotel. We didn't have to pack and repack as most trips require. Each day became more exciting until the last evening when everything came to a crescendo with an unbeliev-able evening usually at a place off limits to the traveling public. Examples of these last nights follow:

Copenhagen, Denmark: The oldest stock exchange in the world was cleared out and made ready for our dinner and dancing. This was the first time in their long history that they made this grand place available to the public.

Rome, Italy: Live, Caesar-like horse chariots entered our hotel's grand ballroom where we had just had a superb dinner. Aboard were "Caesar and his bride." Of course, they were none other than tour members, in togas — Randall and Robbin Tysinger of Thomasville, NC. None of us had seen such in our lives. Commercial tours just do not offer such unique events.

Chapter 12 – Foreign Travel

The most memorable Serta trip for us was the last trip to Vienna, Austria. (We had already been to Vienna on an earlier trip). After a great week consisting of a river cruise on the Danube when the captain of the ship swayed to and fro with the soothing waltz music of Johann Strauss, Jr. — "The Blue Danube"; a fabulous tour of the summer palace of the Hapsburg family; an opera at the world-famous Vienna Opera House; and an afternoon in the unbelievable, crystal-chandeliered arena where we watched the world famous Lippizaner Horses go through their paces. We then came to the final night when we went to the downtown Hapsburg Palace, the most beautiful place that we had ever seen. The evening began in the enormous marble rotunda of the entrance hall where we had cocktails. Next we were ushered into the great dining hall for a seated dinner. If this were not enough, in came the Vienna Boys Choir to sing for us! Afterwards, we went back to the rotunda and out on the spacious stone patio and giant back lawn. Much to our surprise, in came four golden carriages, drawn by teams of four white horses along the huge circular driveway. Aboard were 12 beautiful lady ballet dancers dressed in white gowns along with 12 men dancers dressed in white tails. To our amazement, they performed a most beautiful ballet for us as the orchestra played Viennese music. Never had we witnessed such an evening. I turned to my good friend, John Maness, and said, "John, how do you plan to top this evening on future Serta trips?" John snapped, "I don't have to, this is my last planned trip because I am retiring." What a way to go out! John and Carolyn had pulled so many rabbits out of their hats for us for so many wonderful years, I suppose it was time for them to say goodbye. We still keep in touch with them, but not in the business world. We all thank them for their business talents, their low-keyed charm and great imagination. They are missed. Their successors, however, carry on in much the same way. What did we all do to deserve such marvelous trips? Lucky us!

A Dream to Sell

Our family, so far, has had the privilege of taking some 25 trips and visiting over 35 countries with our friends at Serta Mattress Company. What happy memories we have stored in our minds. To this day, hopefully, we still might be included on their future trips. I should explain why we are still included, even after being retired for 12 years.

It was always my pleasure to write John Maness a thank-you note upon our return from each Serta trip. This is what I was doing just before I was fired from Henredon in 1981. In fact, I had already written the note when the word arrived that I was fired, so I just added a postscript to announce to John what had just happened. The next day, upon receiving my letter, John reached me by telephone. He seemed upset and very surprised. He told me that I should not leave the furniture industry. He insisted that there were many who would hire me. That was comforting to me at a very low time in my life. He told me that our family had been an asset on the trips as well as my having helped him open many new Serta Accounts. He then, probably, went too far. He told me that as long as there was a Serta trip I was welcome to travel with them. I was very much flattered. So far, so good. We still travel with Serta.

The following are the Serta trips that we were privileged to take, in chronological order:

London, England, Scotland and Ireland
Copenhagen, Denmark and Sweden
Costa del Sol, Southern Spain, Gibraltar and North Africa
Rio de Janeiro, Brazil
Rome, Italy
Debrovnic, Yugoslavia
Bern, Switzerland
Munich, Germany

Chapter 12 – Foreign Travel

Lisbon, Portugal

Vienna, Austria and Salzburg

Honolulu (Pearl Harbor), Hawaii

Rome, Italy

Cruise, Southern Caribbean, Mexico

San Francisco and Monterey, California

Maui, Hawaii

Canada: Montreal, Edmonton, Ottawa, Toronto, Quebec

Vienna, Austria

Cruise, Southern Caribbean, Aruba, St. Thomas, St. John, Martinique,
      Venezuela

Lausanne, Switzerland

Monaco on the French Riviera

London, England

Princeville, Hawaii

Cruise, Southern Caribbean, St. Thomas, St. John, St. Martin,
      Barbados

On Thanksgiving 1977, my wife Betty showed me an advertisement from the *Charlotte Observer* by Queens College that had a catchy title, "How Would You Like to Not Have to Decorate for Christmas This Year?" It went on to state that Dr. George Stegner and wife Jackie were planning a wonderful trip to China for three weeks over Christmas and New Year's. Betty told me that she had booked passage for the two of us to go. I had for many years mentioned that I would love to see "old China" before it was spoiled by hordes of tourists. She remembered. The closer the time approached the more Betty had cold feet about leaving our two college-age children with relatives while we traveled together to that ancient land of China. She canceled her trip because the children had said to her, "Mom, we want you to be with us for Christmas. If one parent has to be away, maybe Dad could be the one." Well, I was put into my place quickly. They, too, knew that I was a student of Marco Polo and had a great desire to see China. So around mid-December 1977, before China was officially opened to travelers, I joined the Queens College group for an educational tour, and we departed on what turned out to be a 48,000-mile trip. Pakistan was the only country that China allowed to issue visas, so we had to go through Karachi and spend a couple days. We flew to New York, Paris, France, Germany, and then to Kashmir while in Pakistan. We then flew over the Himalayan Mountains (32,000 feet high) into Beijing, the capital of China.

I mentioned earlier that this trip was sponsored by the National Education Association. Chairman Mao Tse Tung, since 1959, had totally destroyed the educational system of China in order to control his people more strictly. He sent all of the professors to swine farms and brought all the swine farmers to the school system to insure his wishes. By 1977, he realized China, to succeed, must re-establish the educational system. He wanted input from the educational world. Thus, we were invited. We toured all the preschool facilities and the universities. It was amazing how much progress he was making. English was to be the new language, and they set the year 2000 to be first-class citizens of the world.

As I had expected, China was very primitive. The people rushed to our buses to see those strange foreigners. The average age of the national population was 18 due to the fact that Mao had destroyed some fifty million of the older people in order to shape the younger people to his wishes.

Since it was winter we had the best places to stay. The red carpet was out for us. We traveled by buses, trains and their commercial airlines. We were able to see most of China in our two and a half weeks there. Of course, our visit to the Great Wall was very exciting as were Beijing, Shanghai, which was the largest city in the world, and most all of the other major cities. President Nixon and Secretary Kissinger had recently been to China to sign the famous Shanghai Accords that would open China to the world. In that city, we occupied the same apartments that they used while in Shanghai. We departed Shanghai for Beijing to fly back home. Now comes the highlight of our trip! On January 1, 1978, Mao announced that China was open to the world. He invited all Americans in China at the time to a dinner in the Great Hall in Beijing. Only 75 Americans could be found and, our group of 25 were among the guests. It was a very snowy night, with the temperature hovering around zero. What an event! We had no idea that this historical event was to take place while we were in China. A lifetime memory for us all.

On the next trip with Queens College, our entire family went to Egypt and up the Nile River. It was quite a trip, and our two children received college credits which included a test at the end. We departed Egypt for Istanbul, Turkey, that mysterious city that is partly in Europe and partly in Asia. It is also the terminus of the world-famous Orient Express Railroad. We enjoyed the many splendid sights there, including the Great Palaces of the Old Ottoman Empire (when the city went under the name Constantinople) and the famous "Blue Mosque." We crossed the Bosporus into Asia and visited the ancient city of Ephesus where Paul preached and was stoned. All in all, this was a great trip for our family with unbelievable memories for each.

Other trips with Queens College included Australia, New Zealand, Vienna, India-Nepal, Southeast Asia, and London. All the trips were three weeks long and occurred in January, my weakest furniture month. I would like to briefly highlight three of these trips:

India: A most intriguing country that the British could never really rule. India is as old, if not older, than China. Monuments abound. We see on television the mass population of their major cities, Delhi, Bombay and Calcutta, but to our surprise, most of the people live in the country towns. After we had toured most of India, we flew to the remote city of Katmandu, Nepal. This ancient city was not opened to the world until 1950. It is located in the Himalayan Mountains. They have a king and great palaces. Their army is the most savage in the world in that they fight with knives. A detachment of these "Gherkas" guards the Queen of England to this day. From Katmandu, we flew to "Tiger Tops" where the British operate a fabulous resort in a wildlife preserve. We were met at the airstrip by 11 huge elephants that were to take us through deep swamp waters (overflow from the melting snows of the Himalayan Mountains) to "Tiger Tops." A photographer's paradise! The hostesses there were models from around the world, dressed in safari clothes. At night the temperature fell dramatically, so we slept under three wool blankets. We saw exotic animals of every kind, including Bengal tigers, one-horn rhinoceroses and many more. It was an experience of a lifetime!

South America: We traveled to every country in this huge continent in three weeks. We went to bed late and were up long before dawn each day, but we visited 12 countries. I believe the highlight was visiting for two days the second largest waterfalls (behind Victoria Falls in Africa), Iguacu. We had never witnessed such a rainbow- laden scene. We spent the night at an old British hotel where the grounds were alive with varieties of Macaw parrots.

Southeast Asia: Little did we know that this would be Betty's last foreign trip. She would die a year later, much to our sorrow. It was, indeed, a most exotic trip. We visited nine countries: Hong Kong; Singapore; Jakarta, Indonesia; Rangoon and Mandalay, Burma; Bangkok, Thailand; Bali; Java; Fiji Islands; and finally Tahiti. All of these countries were highlights, but I must tell you about a night in the old Strand Hotel in Rangoon, Burma. We all decided to buy and dress in Burmese typical clothing. We met in this out-of-the-past hotel lobby that had the old ceiling fans slowly turning and an old piano that needed to be played. One of our group sat down at the piano to play "On the Road to Mandalay." There were two elderly sisters on our trip who had been professors at Queens College, and they strolled over to the piano and helped us to sing 17 verses of that song. What a scene! I can remember a phrase from one of the verses that went something like this: "Ship me east of the Suez where the flying fishes play — on my way to Mandalay." We all felt that we were back to the time the British ruled this fabled land and Rudyard Kipling was there with us, singing along. Many are the memories that one carries in one's mind from traveling in "faraway places with strange sounding names!"

In all, with Queens College, we traveled on eight trips to more than 40 countries. George and Jackie Stegner are fabulous tour guides. They always hosted our tour group at their home in Charlotte for an orientation and then afterwards to celebrate and dress in the costumes of the countries visited and to eat a gourmet meal fashioned after the special food that we had enjoyed on the trip. Naturally, everyone brought an album of their photos taken on the trip. This was, a beautiful touch which we all enjoyed very much.

Following are the complete trips we took with Queens College:

China: Paris; Germany; Egypt; Dubai; The Oil Emirates; Pakistan, Karachi, Kashmir and The Kyber Pass; China, Beijing, Shanghai and most all of China. (48,000 miles roundtrip.)

Egypt: (Up the Nile River) and Turkey, Istanbul, Ephesus.

Australia; New Zealand and The Fiji Islands: Entire countries.

South America: Brazil, Rio; Paraguay; Uruguay; Argentina, Buenos Aires, Iguacu Water Falls (Second to Victoria in Africa); Bolivia; Chile; Peru, Lima, Cusco (18,000 Feet) and Machu Picchu (the ruined Inca City); Headwaters of the Amazon River; Colombia; Panama and Venezuela.

Austria: Vienna, Danube Cruise; Hungary, Budapest.

India: (Entire country); Nepal, Katmandu; Tiger Tops; Himalayan Mountains and Tibet.

Southeast Asia: Hong Kong; Singapore; Indonesia, Jakarta; Burma, Rangoon and Mandalay; Thailand, Bangkok; Bali; Java; Fiji Islands and Tahiti.

London, England: Most all of England.

A total of eight trips and over 40 countries visited.

We traveled with Duke University on a 21-day cruise to the Greek Islands: Turkey, Istanbul; the Black Sea; Ukraine; Romania, Bucarest; Malta; Yalta; Russia, Odessa and finally to Athens, Greece, to see the Parthenon and then back to New York City and home. We had traveled to nine countries and added these to our memories.

In addition to the above trips, we took some 14 private trips and visited over 10 countries. Highlights from three of these trips are described below:

<u>Russia:</u> In March of 1977, I went to Russia on Japanese Air Lines. The first city was Moscow. Our tour included their marvelous subway system, Red Square, their wonderful circus, their ballet and the countryside. We were there about a week and then took a bad train to St. Petersburg for another week. The architecture there is most impressive, dating back to Peter the Great. The highlight was the Winter Palace with the Hermitage Museum attached. The world's greatest collection of fine art is contained in this museum. The building itself is a work of art. We found the Russian people to be very cold and without any charm. The women did most of the hard work.

<u>Vienna, Austria:</u> We went to celebrate Mozart's 100th anniversary of his death. Each night we had fine Mozart concerts in the cities where he had composed his works: Vienna, Austria; Salzburg, Austria and Prague, Czechoslovakia. We were the first tourists to go to Prague because Russia had just opened the country to visitors. It was very dirty, but one could still see the great architecture that existed prior to Russia's having taken it over after the end of WWII.

<u>China:</u> It had been 23 years since my first trip to China in 1977. For the celebration of the 2000 Millennium, Dixie and I decided to go to China. It would be her first. For me, the country had undergone a vast change towards modernization. Skyscrapers were everywhere to be seen. Their airports were modern and mostly made of marble. The people seemed very happy and contented. We toured the whole country: Beijing; The Great Wall; Terracotta Soldiers; The Yangtze River Cruise (longest river in China flowing some 4,000 miles) and Shanghai, where we were lucky enough to get a room in the newly

renovated Peace Hotel on the Bund. It was a great experience for Dixie, who is interested in every form of art. For me, I could not believe the giant strides China had made into the 21st century. I do believe they have surpassed their goal of 1977 to become a first-class nation of the world. Watch out, America, China is coming!

In summary of our private foreign travel, we took 14 trips and visited more than 10 countries:

Jamaica: Five trips (three with family and two as a furniture consultant to the Jamaican government).

Russia (1977): Moscow, St. Petersburg; Finland.

London, England: four trips.

Vienna and Salzburg, Austria; Prague, Czechoslovakia.

Germany: Entire country; Basal; Luxembourg and France.

China (2000): Entire country including the Yangtze River Cruise.

Canadian Rockies: Calgary, Lake Louise, Banff Springs and Jasper.

Lastly, I could not omit my grand trip, complements of the U.S. Army, to the South Asian Command in the South Pacific for two years. First to Australia, New Guinea and on to the Philippine Islands: Bagio, Bataan, Corregidor, Manila. One trip and I visited three countries. This was a no-frills trip with a war thrown in for good measure. Postscript: We won that war over there!

The grand total for foreign travel, so far, is 48 trips to more than 96 countries. With my more than 2.6 million miles traveled by auto in my 44 years of business travel, one would think I like to travel. I do, and I enjoyed it all to the max. Travel expands your mind and enlarges your horizons. Do you have a trip to offer? In addition to the foreign travel cited, I have traveled to more than 60 major cities in the U.S.A.

I must say, in writing this chapter, I have revisited all of these wonderful foreign places and reinvigorated my memories. As I wrote, I was reminded of the great WWII song: "Faraway places with strange sounding names." I never, in my fondest dreams, thought that I would be privileged to such a treat. How most fortunate and blessed our family is to have had these opportunities to travel. Travel is an excellent investment in that one cannot lose the memories. The stock market can go up and down, real estate can fluctuate, but memories last forever. "Life is uncertain, so eat your dessert first!"

One can see that we have been a very busy family. Busy people stay young. Activity stimulates the body and mind. I would like to do it all over again — as in the old Humphrey Bogart movie *Casablanca*, when Bogie said to the piano player, "Play it again, Sam!"

Thanks, again, to my childhood friend Bob Small for his excellent advice about "taking the time along the way to smell the roses."

Bon voyage!

CHAPTER 13

Retirement

A Dream to Sell

nlike most, I was not looking forward to retirement. I had the best job I could have hoped for. Honestly, I could not believe that I received fat checks each month for the fun that I was having. For something that I loved dearly, could I simply walk away from it so abruptly? Friends in the business were taking bets that I would return. This made the decision to retire even more taxing for me. I was 64 years of age, in excellent health and loved what I was doing.

I took a look at Pete Rose in professional baseball who was up to his neck in a gambling controversy and it appeared he would never be asked to be in baseball's Hall of Fame. He had had a most excellent career and certainly deserved such a recognition. I related this to my own career. I had always heard the time to quit is when you are at the pinnacle of your career at or near your retirement age. I had just reached my life's goal in sales. This was a home run, and the people in the stands were cheering. It was the time for me to leave the park. Pete Rose should have done this earlier, before the scandal. This answered my question as to the timing of my retirement. I also learned that possibly there would be adjustments in my territory. I had been down that road too many times in the past. Now, what to do?

Even though I had taught adult Sunday school classes for some 38 years, chaired every committee in our church, First United Methodist, High Point, served on our Western N.C. District and was currently a member of our Bishop's Blue Ribbon Committee to revitalize older churches, I still thought my time for all charities was limited due to my massive travel schedule. At that point, I decided that I would give 10 years of my retirement to charities. After all, time is the most valuable gift one can give to a cause. I also remembered what the Bible has to say regarding this: "For those who are given much, more is expected."

To be effective, one has to believe strongly about which charities to select to give his effort. My great longtime friend and neighbor, Fred Alexander, then president of High Point Bank and Trust, helped me on one to be selected — the High Point Salvation Army. He simply picked me up at my home and took me to a monthly meeting. I had been involved with Duke University and its School of Forestry for some time and was on their advisory board since 1988. The school had been one of the best in the past, but was in need of revitalization. Since I had been a part of using up much lumber in the manufacturing of furniture, I thought that I needed to help in ways to restore the forest. So I decided to select that charity to give of my time and treasure. The last charity that I selected was Lees-McRae College, a struggling little private Presbyterian college in Banner Elk, NC which was founded almost a hundred years ago, at the time, by the Rev. Edgar Tufts. Betty had worked her way through that two-year school right after WWII. We had already given a scholarship in her name. So, this school became the third charity that I selected. There is a later chapter on charities in which I will discuss this subject more fully.

So I was beginning to get part of my retirement schedule together. But, "all work and no play makes Jack a dull boy." I needed to really get to know my neighbors. I needed to cultivate new friends and renew old friendships. My old college buddy and fraternity brother Bob Hauser organized a Dixieland jazz band and asked me to join. He assigned me to the one-string bass, better known as "gut bucket." All members were in our church, so we decided we would play gigs and use our proceeds to help underwrite our church's television ministry. Our compensation was the massive fun we were to have. We named ourselves "The Little Booger Band." The following persons were members: Bob Hauser, on the "eighty-eight"; Tommy Gray, trombone; Mark Pierce, trumpet; Charles Bryan, trumpet; Bill Struss, trombone; Ray Wardell, drums; and Plato Wilson on the "gut bucket." From time to time we had the following singers: Joe Huff, Jack Cecil and finally Perry McDowell. We averaged approximately 20 gigs a year for eight years. Some were free performances to help worthy charities to raise money, such as Hospice, the Salvation Army and others. We played weddings, anniversaries, birthdays, dances, store grand openings and for anyone who had a telephone to call us. I was the bookie of all the gigs. This job took time. Bob Hauser wrote all of our musical arrangements for each instrument, except mine. I always felt left out! I think we must have raised more than $35,000 for our church and had $100,000 worth of fun. Our most distant gig was to Goldsboro, NC to play for a New Orleans evening at their country club. We thought ourselves "famous." Others would have to decide that.

I had tried all of my life to play golf and absolutely could not play the game. When I was growing up, I took care of two clay tennis courts for wealthy people in town. Part of my compensation was to be allowed to learn to play on the courts. I was fair but dropped the game as my life began to be busy. Thirty-five years later, after my horseback days, I decided to go back to tennis. I loved it and could get a good workout in just an hour and a half. I was still working when this happened. My good friend, Jack Greer and I joined Jim Hayworth and his son, Jimmy, in doubles play at Oak Hollow Tennis Center. Jim was a former high school tennis coach and a superb athlete. He was an excellent instructor but a taskmaster. We had fun, and I realized when I retired I would like to play more tennis.

At Gingercake, where we spent our summers, we needed a new tennis court, and it fell to me to raise the money to build it. I thought $10,000 would get this accomplished. We had a rather wealthy summer resident who I thought might make this new court possible. I contacted him in Florida and outlined the need. I asked him for $10,000, and he immediately responded that he would give that amount. As it turned out, it would cost close to $18,000 to complete. I was back on the phone asking this gentleman, Herb Peyton, for more. He said, "Sorry Plato, you've just learned a vital lesson in fund-raising — ask for what you need the first time!" He didn't give anymore, so I had to pass the hat among the other residents. I relate this story in order to tell you about the great tennis that we all had in the summers at Gingercake. These are some of the spirited players we had there: John Hopper, Cass Sumrall, Mark Senter, Frank and Renate Leister, Mac and Helen Patton, Nancy and Clark Hatcher, David Cole and Ed Neff. Guests were invited to play in special events. Much fun for everyone! Of course, the court's name is the Peyton Court.

High Point Country Club built two beautiful courts at the inside tennis facility at Willow Creek that afforded winter tennis. This was a good place to stay in shape and enjoy tennis during those long winter months. We had a spirited foursome, in spite of some of our mature ages, which included Percy Idol, Frank Sizemore, Jack Greer and myself. Tall tales and other world-solving stories abounded after the games. One day I picked up Percy Idol for the ride to Willow Creek to play tennis and Percy off-handedly remarked, "We really play like professionals." I was shocked and asked, "In what way?" Percy came back with, "We play injured all the time!" I think that Percy got that right in that most seniors often play that way.

I later joined and am currently a part of another tennis foursome that offered bigger challenges and made us all better players. "Spirited" is a mild name for our play! "Losing" is not a word in the vocabulary of our foursome. This fact is what makes our playing so much fun and at the same time lifted our games to a higher level sometimes. Playing tennis with friends you really like, off and on the court, is a marvelous experience and fun at its best. If one is not up to his game on a given day, he will soon be advised in a friendly way of the fact by silence, a stare, or even a comment. This indeed will focus one to raise his game to a higher level. That is what sports are all about. With everyone having busy schedules and travel plans, we usually start the winter season with six players on the team in order to always have four to play on our scheduled day. It is the responsibility of the absent member to arrange his own substitute so as to insure the foursome. Our current players are David Dowdy, Jim Millis, Hunter Dalton, Cal Anderson and Herb "Turbo" Adkins. Doris Dowdy, a superb tennis player, sometimes fills-in for someone. She really lifts our grade of play.

It has been Dixie's and my pleasure, on two occasions, to invite some of our tennis group up to "Timbuktu" at Gingercake, as many as our house would accommodate, for weekends to play tennis and socialize. We wish that we had a larger house to accommodate all. On these occasions much fun and laughter abounded. We cooked outside, went to special restaurants, played tennis and generally had a relaxing time. Friends are special! The wives always enjoyed shopping in Blowing Rock. I must say, the wives are the best part of the tennis group. The couples who were able to come to our summer home were Doris and David Dowdy, Jesse and Jim Millis and Sue and Cal Anderson. One of these visits was in October, and the weather turned pretty chilly. Eating out on our patio was a sight. We loaned everyone heavy jackets and extra sweaters. We all looked like a snow patrol! But the steaks were delicious. If that were not enough, the power went out as did our heat. We just built a fire in the big fireplace, and all was well. Events such as these only add to the memories. Retirees aren't supposed to have this much fun!

Another special event was the tennis outing that the Millises and Andersons offered at their vacation retreats at Litchfield in South Carolina. Because of a death in our family, Dixie and I could not attend. We understand that everyone else had a ball and enjoyed every minute of the weekend. Jesse and Jim later had us all down to their farm near High Point where Jesse really outdid herself with an evening of homemade food and happy memories. We have fun on and off the courts.

Reunions are a wonderful way to keep in touch with families and friends. In retirement, we all have the time to organize and put together such events. Since 1980, our family has tried to have a reunion every two years, and we have them at our mountain cottage where all the memories began back in 1950. Even though children and grandchildren have scattered far and wide, we gather every other summer on the first weekend in August. We usually have 100 percent attendance that represents family in North Carolina, South Carolina, Florida and Alabama. They scatter, but they stay in the South! It is a grand time to visit, catch up on happenings in our lives, and simply have a good time reliving memories.

I was fortunate enough to have gone to high school with a fantastic class of outstanding friends. We graduated at the beginning of WWII in 1943, just in time to serve our great country in that war. The men all went directly into the various armed services and left all those pretty girls at home, never knowing what was to happen to them as we shipped out all over the world. It took a 40th class reunion in 1983 to find out what happened to the girls. Many of them headed to Washington, DC, and took wartime jobs there as secretaries and some in the State Department where they were key players in the war, speaking several languages. Still others went on to college and excelled. It was wonderful to see how well they had done without us. I was the one given the job of getting our classmates to these reunions which we had: 40th (1983); 45th (1988); 50th (1993) and 57th (2000) — our millennium. Most of us in 1943 never believed we would ever witness the millennium, yet most of us were there at the 57th reunion almost as young looking as when we graduated. Someone dubbed us a class "forever young." We were able to get large numbers of the 154 who graduated to come and enjoy each other for these four reunions. It was all very much fun for all. We are forever united! We usually did much of the planning for these reunions at Gingercake, which holds many fond memories, over patio dinners.

In 1997, after 47 years of cramped living and much entertaining, I thought it was time to remodel again and to enlarge our unique and memorable little cottage. I drew up the plans that included adding two more bedrooms, four more closets, another bathroom and central heat. Virgil Barrier, a local construction contractor, took on the job. He and his crew did a superb job. Later they remodeled the kitchen for us. Since the décor in the house was so unusual, I decided to furnish the new portion in Chinese antiques and accessories. It was much fun and has been enjoyed by many who have been guests. Even the rainbow trout in the stream that flows though our lawn have enjoyed all the guests who feed them well.

In July 1997, I was introduced by a friend to a beautiful lady Dixie Propst of Morganton, my hometown. She had moved to Morganton after I had left there. At the same time it was my pleasure to meet her only son David, his wife Jennifer, and their two daughters Hannah and Gabrielle. Dixie and I were greatly attracted to each other. We enjoyed our courtship very much and later, on October 17, 1998, we chose a quaint little stone Presbyterian Church, 100 years old, in Crossnore near Gingercake to be married. It was a very small but happy wedding with family and a few close friends in attendance. We all had dinner afterwards at the Eseeola Lodge in Linville. She is and has been the love of my life. Her great fashion skills have even brought mine up a notch or two. She loves flowers and as a result, our summer cottage abounds with beautiful flowers. Dixie is a lovely lady to enhance my retirement. For our honeymoon, we chose to go to London for a week and then we toured by automobile a 100-mile radius of London, spending the nights in famous old estate homes. If traveling with Dixie was not enough excitement, the driving on the left side in the automobile was. In addition, we have had the opportunity to travel together to Hawaii, on a Caribbean cruise, and for the millennium, on an extensive three-week trip to China. The latter was a very long trip, but we came back with our heads full of happy memories of that far-off place with strange sounding names. Dixie is a beautiful lady in all ways!

One cannot believe the activities that are offered to the summer guests who visit the mountains of western North Carolina near our summer home. There is in the area first-class entertainment available two or three nights a week. Lees-McRae College has its summer "Forum" which features eight outstanding programs that would be a credit to a major city. In addition, their world-class performing arts department offers at least four wonderful plays a summer. The famous and multi-talented Janet Spears is responsible for these productions. She is a national treasure for Lees-McRae College and the "summer people." There is "the Appalachian Summer" series sponsored by Appalachian State University. One should not miss these extraordinary performances. Then, there are the many waterfalls, hiking trails, and spectacular views on the Blue Ridge Parkway. Not to be left out is the marvelous cool weather. No wonder too many people are discovering this paradise. A great place to spend the hot months for your retirement!

Back in High Point for our winters, we have caring and wonderful immediate neighbors in the Cargals (Paige, Steve, Dillon and Chase); Kuhns (Bob, Kathy and David); Jane and Harry Price; Alice and Harrison Rucker; and Ursula Hafele. We all look after each other and they, especially, watch over our house when we travel and spend the summers away. It's great to have good neighbors.

Since 1980, we have been members of "the supper club" in which we have enduring and best friends: Betty and Bob Hauser; Betty and Martin Keaton; Jo and Walter Jones; Mutt and Harold McGee; and

A Dream to Sell

Jean and Dave Wagoner. Yeararound, we have a group dinner usually the first Friday night of each month. When you do this for 22 years, you get to know and love each other very much. There is nothing that each of us would not do for the other. Friends and tradition count!

Too much of my time is still spent managing various investments during my retirement. I suppose that I deserve this task in that I put them together in my earlier life. The old adage is probably true: "Death, taxes and change are constant." I can handle very well all of these but the first one. At 77 years young, I don't have the time to think about that.

Retirement is wonderful. One still is very busy, but the pace is of one's own choosing. Sleeping late is a luxury for Dixie and me. Not too many neckties and suits make for a much more comfortable lifestyle as well. It's a time to know your neighbors and cultivate new and old friendships. For the life of me, I cannot imagine getting senior discounts. I hate to be disloyal to my fellow seniors, but I think the discounts should go to the young, on their way up, raising families and paying for homes. We seniors have done all that and have more marbles that we have collected in a lifetime. However, if they insist, we will accommodate the grantors. So far so good has been my retirement. I look forward to many more wonderful years to enjoy in good health with my wonderful wife Dixie!

CHAPTER 14

Charities

A Dream to Sell

At a very young age, 10 or 12 perhaps, while I was working for my uncle Harry Wilson, I noticed something very special about him, and it made an impression on me, especially as he was one of my mentors. As he sat with his business leaders and talked about current events, I noted that when the conversation turned to the two state institutions that were in Morganton, Uncle Harry would rally and be very passionate in his remarks. This was because he was proud to serve on the boards of these two fine facilities. These were the North Carolina School for the Deaf and the State Hospital for the Mentally Ill, now Broughton Hospital. He was appointed to these boards for his leadership abilities and partly for his political leadership as a Democrat in Burke County — he delivered the vote to the party! More than that, he was proud of these most worthy institutions and was genuinely interested in and passionate about their effectiveness. As a result of his many years on these boards, he was effective in helping the institutions receive ample funds from the state to insure proper leadership and to see that they were kept in up-to-date order. His passion stemmed from no other reason. He was their watchdog! I learned then and there that it must be a good feeling to give something back to worthy causes. This experience stayed with me for the rest of my life.

As discussed earlier, in my chapter "Retirement," I felt it was time for me to give something back. The Bible prescribes: "For those who are given much, more is expected of them." I believe that Americans are basically charitable. I have learned, however, that giving is not a natural instinct but the reverse, one of survival and preservation. Giving is an instinct that must be cultivated. My experience is that once cultivated, giving becomes a habit and is much easier to do.

At this moment, my mind flashes back to my father who had some bad habits along with a very good one: He had feelings for those less fortunate than he. This feeling manifested itself in two rather unconventional ways: (1) Seldom on Sunday mornings did he not get a telephone call from the local jail that one or several of his employees had partied too much on Saturday night and had been taken to jail. The jailer asked my father if he would "go on their bond" in order for their release. So, on his way to take us three children to Sunday school, we stopped by the jail to "free the prisoners." For years I thought the jail was a part of the Methodist Church! Of course, my father later paid their court costs with the provision that his employees would reimburse him, which they very seldom did. (2) My father had more friends across the county than most anybody. They ran the scale between poor and those of means. Invariably, it was those without means who approached him for loans. Many of these paid back little or none of these loans. My daddy was not dumb in these matters; it was simply his method of giving to charity. Most of the times he, himself, was without much means, but that did not matter when others were in worse shape than he. The loans were paid off in full on the occasion of his death and funeral when the church was overflowing and the grounds around the church were full as well. They all had come to thank him for deeds done for them, and to salute a friend of theirs. We, as a family, wondered what our favorite pastor Fletcher Nelson would have to say on behalf of our sometime-wayward father and husband. The heart of the remarks went something like this: "Ab (Albert) was a friend of the people. His charity was shown in a Christian way throughout his life. His appreciation is shown in the vast numbers who have bothered to come and pay their last respects to him as their dear friend." Charity reveals itself in many strange ways. Thank you, Dad, for showing me the many aspects of charity!

The dictionary has something to say about one who is charitable: spiritual; benevolent; Christian love; best side of a person; kindly;

compassionate; loving and considerate. My, what lofty ideals to have to practice daily! These are not a checklist, only traits that are found in persons who always have a feeling for others.

Have you ever asked yourself, "Who am I?" It's a risky question to answer. At the risk of getting my answer wrong to this question, here goes: I am conservative; hard working; trying to be a Christian and somewhat overly organized. I am developing into a much more charitable person. It took some cultivating by Jack Slane and Perry Keziah some years ago to teach me how to be more charitable. In the latter part of my career, with a little success, I felt like the dog that actually caught the garbage truck and didn't know what to do with it. Another mentor, Henry Wilson, told me once, "I don't get too excited over money, but unfortunately, that's how Americans keep score." Nearing retirement age, I felt the need to serve charities and lend to them any abilities I could offer.

After much consideration, I chose these charities to give my time, talents and treasure:

The Salvation Army: This is a unique and Christian worldwide organization that was founded in 1864 in London, England, by William Booth, a Methodist minister. His original mission has not changed to this day. It simply is to find unfortunate persons, at the time of their worst need, and help them in a Christian way until they can arrange to be on their own. This is done by education and counseling, and their faith is optional, but usually they choose it for life. Their track record is outstanding. The Salvation Army is the No. 1 charity in America as to contributions received. And what is even more important is that almost 90 percent of gifts reach the needy persons. This is twice the record of most such charities. They do not toot their horns about their services in that they are a Christian organization staffed by ordained ministers. They truly are the first on the scene in any emergencies and the last to leave, only to care for the harmed later by counseling and financial aid.

You can easily see that this charity is worthy of your and my support. I joined them in 1990.

Duke University's Nicholas School of the Environment: This worthwhile endeavor, when I joined their advisory board in 1987, was the Duke University Graduate School of Forestry. Originally only Duke and Yale had such schools. Later, many other schools were developed across America, and the unique effectiveness of Duke's school was challenged. It was my privilege to help formulate a broader new school with uniqueness factors. The solution was fathered by the Duke biology dean, Norm Christensen. He laid out the vision of a new school that encompassed the entire environment. We knew that he had the answer. In addition, of the $55 million needed to establish the new school and the building to house it, he contacted former students of his, Mr. and Mrs. Nicholas of Boston Scientific and Eli Lily Drug Company, also trustees of Duke University, and they gave $20 million towards the transition of the school. What a hero was Norm Christensen! I continued on board to see the completion of the new school and building to the joy of all concerned. Now Duke has a state of the arts environmental school that is helping the world be a much better place in which to live. Of course, the new school is named Duke's Nicholas School of the Environment. In 2002, Norm chose to step down from the school's first deanship in order to return as a professor in the classroom. I also chose, after 15 years on their advisory board, to retire from that board in the same year. It was a rewarding tour of duty. After all, we all need a great environment.

Lees-McRae College: My connection to this little private Presbyterian college, founded by the Rev. Edgar Tufts in 1900, goes back to 1946 when my wife-to-be, Betty Cashion, worked her way through this two-year college. Also, my dear friend the Rev. Fletcher Nelson, a Methodist minister, and former minister to our family, was persuaded to be president of the three identities of the Tuft's Memorial

Foundation: Lees-McRae College, Cannon Memorial Hospital and the Grandfather Orphanage. I knew of the great work that these institutions were doing. Later, the three were separated and Lees-McRae College, as were the other two, became independent. So in 1990, the year of my retirement, I was asked to serve on their board of trustees. I did so for one four-year term and then chose not to be re-nominated. After being off for three years, I was asked again to serve a second term, which ended in 2002. I again requested not to be re-nominated. I was stressed out on the hard work while serving there. One cannot begin to understand the hard decisions trustees have to make in directing a small private school. At 77, I thought that I needed some retirement for Dixie and me. After all, I had more than satisfied the 10 years that I had pledged of my time to charities. I still choose to continue my work with the Salvation Army.

For me, there were at least two aspects for serving on charity boards: One can shape long-lasting policies and lend financial support to the less fortunate. The results of serving: (1) a very warm heart and, (2) frustration due to too many fellow board members serving just for the honor, rubber-stamping too many proposals without the passion to seek the right, hard solutions. Popularity was more important than hammering out those proper solutions. While serving on these boards, I did have the opportunity of meeting many exceptional people whom I am privileged to call my friends.

Earlier on, I was privileged to chair the following charitable fund campaigns:

First United Methodist Church's Renovation Campaign: This was a $600,000 campaign which we were successful in raising. For the first time, our church accepted corporate gifts to the campaign.

Two or three every-member canvasses for raising the church's annual budget. The budgets were anywhere from $300,000 to $400,000. I must tell you a true story that I experienced in a call to one of our members. I chose what I thought was an affluent member to call on first. When I arrived at the up-scale home, I saw two late-model automobiles and a deluxe boat in the driveway. I just knew this was going to be a big pledge. When I was allowed in, I found the home well furnished. I stated my reason for being there. They simply said that they really could not afford to make a pledge for this year. I was stunned! Dejected, I returned to the church and confessed to our pastor that I had struck out and explained the circumstances. The pastor said, "No wonder they cannot afford to pledge, they already have pledged too much for their pleasures." This didn't help me too much nor the campaign. I was learning — big time. Some people have different priorities in their lives. I'm glad to announce that all three of the budgets were subscribed.

Gingercake's new club house: This was only a $30,000 campaign but only a few to give. We did this successfully.

Peyton Tennis Court at Gingercake: I have earlier told of the details of this campaign. The goal was $20,000 of which my friend Herb Peyton Sr., gave half. We were successful in having that wonderful tennis court that has been enjoyed for years.

The Greater High Point Salvation Army Endowment: In 1995, I was serving on the Salvation Army's social concerns committee which Bob Parrish chaired. One day Bob asked the committee if we were going to be active this year or just operate normally. I spoke up, since I was a new member, and said that I thought we should always be active. Bob then said, "We need to raise some money." I suggested that we establish an endowment that would satisfy all the needs of the army in High Point during lean years. Everyone there agreed and asked what dollar amount did I have in mind for the campaign. I said, "If we are going to the well, I think we should get enough water to last a long time. I think we should go for five million dollars." Well, almost everyone fainted! They had in mind a couple hundred thousand dollars for our goal. Of course, I was made the chairman to raise these funds. We organized the campaign into two parts: (1) a cash amount, and (2) a deferred portion (wills, IRA gifts, CRT, etc.). I appointed Ray Edwards to head up the cash campaign and I would, in addition to being overall chairman, conduct the deferred portion. We set the goals for each portion: Cash—$200,000 and Deferred—$4,800,000. We brought in an expert tax attorney, Conrad Teitell, who had conducted seminars for the national Salvation Army earlier. We had two sessions — one for attorneys and CPA's and the other for the general public. The seminars were highly successful. Many lawyers and CPA's directed their clients to the Salvation Army Endowment, due certainly to our pristine image and fine works. I sought out many friends who I thought would like to support this worthy cause. I called on Bill Lepole of our Divisional Headquarters in Charlotte for his expert help on complicated details. Our campaign lasted one year. Since I was retired and it was my idea, it fell to me to make many of the calls. I received cash gifts as well as deferred ones. The final tally was: Cash—$300,000 and Deferred—$8,400,000. Our local Salvation Army, at the Bi-Annual National Salvation Army meeting in California, was presented their "best practices" award for the nation for this innovative campaign. None other than our former commanding officer in High Point, Col. Tom Jones, presented the award to Captain O'Bryan and me. Just to visit with Tom and Mary Jones was worth the whole effort! What I learned from this exciting experience of raising money for the Salvation Army was: Think big, work very hard and have a great product. Our town of greater High Point rallied around the flag for this one. Thanks to all!

Being on the boards of Duke and Lees-McRae College, we all helped in their campaigns to raise funds: Duke's Nicholas School of the Environment $55 million; Lees-McRae College $18,745,000. I'm glad to report that these lofty goals, for each school, have been reached. There is much money out there if you have the heart to go for it.

Chapter 14 – Charities

I would like to recall two projects that I had the pleasure of being involved in, even though they were not charities:

The fight before we built our present new High Point Country Club: Our building a new clubhouse was long overdue. But, what happened in the process was not a very pretty picture. The club was divided on whether it should be at our original in-town location or at our newly acquired location out of town at Willow Creek. Most of us thought that the members would destroy the club in the process. It was like the Civil War! I was playing tennis one day with Bob Amos, Jim Millis and John Wall, and we were discussing this awful war. I spoke up with my solution. The current officers had almost forced the decision on everyone that the club would be rebuilt in town. These officers had not allowed much, if any, input into the matter. Members right and left were going to drop out of the club, causing it to have insufficient funds to build or maintain the new clubhouse. It was nasty and full of emotions. I suggested that the president of the club, Maurice Hull, needed to appoint a blue ribbon committee to hear both sides of the membership, in view of the fact that the management had already lost its credibility. This committee must be made up of true leaders and well-respected people of our city and also members of the club.

My fellow tennis buddies thought this might work. They suggested that I go to Hull and give him the good news. Still in my tennis clothes, I went directly to his law office and told him of my plan, for no other reason than to save his backside and the club itself. He thought it was a great idea. I turned to leave as my job of a delivery boy was completed. He said, "Wait a minute, I want you to chair this committee and select the committee members." I said, "Maurice, I'm not your man, you can find many who are much more qualified, and besides, you need to select your committee members yourself." He called in his law partner, Perry Keziah, and explained the plan. Then, both Perry and Maurice began to sell me on the job. I kept insisting that I was not their man. But I finally relented and accepted this huge responsibility. I dreaded calling my distinguished list of potential committee members, for it read like "who's who" in High Point. Of the 18 called, I had 100 percent acceptance, much to my surprise. As it turned out, everyone was concerned and thought this was our last hope of saving the club. We had only 10 days to complete our mission before the final vote by the club members. Four quick meetings were scheduled, at times every member could attend at least one session at which we just listened to their frustrations. I decided that I would record all of their concerns. When our committee sat, it was truly a distinguished group with the exception of me. We heard them out and were genuinely interested in what they had to say, and they knew it. We settled them down, and the club vote carried to build in town. I think we saved the club. God gave us two ears and one mouth so we could listen twice as much as we talk. His original design really paid off for the committee in bringing this serious matter to a successful conclusion. Listening is a great talent — always!

Since I had spent a lifetime in the furniture business, Jim Morgan called on me to chair the furnishings committee to secure all of the draperies, furniture and accessories for the new club. Our architectural firm in Texas furnished us with the services of their experienced interior designer, which helped very much. My first call was on Ron Jones, CEO of MASCO, who by now owned most of our furniture industry. I made this simple pitch to him: "Mr. Jones, High Point, as you know, is the center of the furniture world. Our buyers come from all over the world twice a year. Our country club is the center for your entertaining. How would you like a permanent display of your products in our brand new club house?" Ron fired back instantly. "We will allow you to select whatever you desire from any of our factories at a 40 percent discount from our cost. You know we own Robert Allen Fabrics (the foremost fabric line in America) so, you can get your drapery fabrics as well at the same discount. MASCO would like to pledge

$25,000 towards your expenses, in addition." I followed up and asked him if his factory trucks would deliver the products to our clubhouse at no charge. He agreed this would be done. I thanked him and departed, 10 feet tall! This formula would be the guideline for other resources that I would contact. It worked like a charm. Our club saved a ton on furnishing the new building. I salute Ron Jones and his companies for making this possible. We were able to select the best furniture in America at a fraction of its cost. We were ready for the worldwide furniture buyers to visit our new country club. It was a win-win situation for all of us. This was not a charity, but close to it. I had much fun doing this for High Point.

In my opinion, the best investment our family ever made in charities was giving a Trinity Scholarship to Duke University in 1986. We had plenty of help from Jack Slane, Perry Keziah and Duke's John Piva in this opportunity. Jack and Perry had lobbied President Terry Sanford of Duke to enroll more North and South Carolinians at Duke since the Duke family originally formed that school for these states. Sanford told them to arrange some scholarships and that he would match them with Ben Duke Scholarships. Jack and Perry thought too many gifted students from North Carolina, and especially the Triad, were going to Ivy League schools and never returning home to help our area progress. Jack and Marsha Slane joined Jack's sister, Doris Slane, to give two of the scholarships. Our family gave the third one. Herman Bernard, who had leanings toward UNC, gave the fourth one. Perry and his family joined the tri-county to give a fifth one. Following were the Cassell-Sapperstein families, then living in High Point, now in Greensboro, who gave the sixth one. This may be the record for the most Trinity Scholarships in any city. The Trinity Scholarship is the best one granted by Duke. It is a four-year award, with all expenses paid, foreign studies and other amenities presented to the winning student. As a by-product, many more students from our area have enrolled at Duke. The

Carolinas have increased from approximately six percent of Duke's enrollment to the present approximately 15 percent. For the original contribution made by each of us, we are assured of having six Trinity Scholarships every four years as long as there is a Duke University. What a bargain! Each grantor has no input into which student is selected as this is done solely by Duke.

In addition, our family has given a Betty C. Wilson Scholarship to Lees-McRae College. We also contribute yearly to two other most worthy scholarships: Tom Haggai and Nido Quebein Associates. I feel very strongly in the merits of preparing young people for a better future for them as well as society in general. I feel grateful for my free college education that was afforded me by the taxpayers of America.

From my own experience in fund-raising for charities, I have found some "do's" and "don'ts":

"DO'S":
1. In the beginning, identify prime givers and approximate gifts.
2. Obtain the right person to call on individuals.
3. Set a deadline for all calls to be made.

"DON'TS":
1. Insist on no telephone calls for the solicitation.
2. Do not announce exactly what your appointment is about.
3. Do not use solicitors who do not have passion for the cause.

Through trial and error, I rediscovered the 80/20 theory. At the end of financial campaigns, I most always found that 80 percent of the gifts were from 20 percent of the givers. I was familiar with this theory from my business experience: 80 percent of my sales of fabrics, frames and casegoods came from 20 percent of the line offered. Consequently, on future campaigns, I worked backwards and started with the results of past campaigns. Example:

The goal of $357,500

1	$25,000 Gift	$25,000
1	$20,000 Gift	$20,000
1	$15,000 Gift	$15,000
6	$10,000 Gifts	$60,000
15	$5,000 Gifts	$75,000
30	$2,500 Gifts	$75,000
50	$1,000 Gifts	$50,000
50	$250 Gifts	$12,500
204	Gifts	$357,500

We then knew how to proceed and who to contact. I used this exact example above in 1985, to raise the funds needed to acquire a parking lot that joined our First United Methodist Church in High Point.

Mrs. Delos Hedgecock had inherited the Sheraton Hotel and parking lot from her late husband. She had tax problems. Through our mutual CPA, David Sledge, we asked her not to cut the price of the parking lot as the price seemed to be a fair one, but rather, would she like to make the first contribution of $25,000 to the church's financial campaign to pay for the parking lot? She said that she would like to do this. She would be entitled to a $25,000 tax deduction. So, I then made up a cardboard chart that revealed how we could raise the $357,500. I called a very special meeting at our church and invited members who I thought would find their place on the chart and make a pledge that night. Never did I tell anyone what the very special meeting was about. They all arrived, and I uncovered the chart. I presented the campaign and quickly told them that they didn't have to worry about the first two large gifts in that they had already been pledged. A sigh of relief came from the crowd. I then related an experience that I had had in my youth when I was milking four cows twice daily. I explained that all four cows knew exactly which was their own feed trough and came there at milking time. I then asked them to find their own trough and consider making their gift to the campaign. Always, the toughest decision for a giver is the amount to give. We helped them with the chart. People knew in their hearts what they ought to give, and this time they would honor their hearts. We were successful that one night with raising the "big money" from a few. Running down the smaller givers took much time and effort.

While on the Board of Trustees at Lees-McRae College during the planning of their latest "New Era" financial campaign, I suggested this 80/20 theory. It was adopted and I am happy to announce that the $18,750,000 goal has been reached. This method puts some science and experience together to bring success.

In my experience while raising funds for various causes, I think I have an opinion of what the mindset of a giver might be, in general. A fund-raiser must understand this mindset in order to obtain results. Please understand that what follows are my own views. I understand many will not agree and especially some givers. Here goes!

The "Darker Side" of motivation to give:
1. For show.
2. Ego reasons.
3. To impress others rather than "for others."
4. For tax deductions.

The Honest Christian Motivation to Share:
1. A pure heart.
2. Concerns for others.
3. Religious responsibility.
4. Plain goodness.

Admitted or not, tax deductions enter into the giver's mind. It's a fact of reality. Surprising to most, the 80/20 theory is evident, in my opinion, as to the motivation of giving: 80 percent consider the tax deduction desirable while 20 percent do not consider the deduction necessary in their giving. At least, this has been my experience. This is one reason that America will never be able to establish a flat tax system. It would be devastating to all charities like churches, schools, hospitals and many more worthy causes.

I have an interesting story to relate regarding my dear and trusted friend and former pastor, Dr. Howard Allred. Incidentally, Howard is a first-rate fund raiser. Howard came to our church at a very low time in our history. He was the right man to revive us in every way. One of the many things he did for us was to suggest that we needed to honor our sanctuary and boost our spirits by renovating it. He went on to say that he didn't envision a churchwide financial campaign, but rather an informal one by him from the pulpit. I was put on the decorating committee, and we came to the conclusion that the cost would be $100,000 to $150,000. I further told Howard of the method that the founder of Lees-McRae College, Edgar Tufts, had used to raise the funds to construct stone buildings on his campus. Mr. Tufts figured out how much a ton of rocks, hauled and put into the building, cost. In 1925, that was $4.00 a ton. He then went out to find out how many tons of rock a person wanted to give to the college building fund. He was very successful and built many beautiful stone buildings on his campus. As Mr. Tufts said, "Everyone wants a bargain!"

I told Howard that he should do the same with our renovation of the sanctuary. Find out how many gallons of paint, applied; how many yards of carpet, installed; and the price of the six chandeliers needed would cost. Howard thought this was an excellent idea and proceeded in his own way to do just this. In a very short time, he had our money to pay for the turnkey job without any time-consuming financial campaign. Congratulations to Howard Allred and our congregation! This is yet another way to raise money.

A Dream to Sell

We all have been inspired by persons who have given willingly to many great causes that have enhanced all of our lives. I have known quite a few. Our family has arrived at our choice for the real prototypes of classic philanthropy. They are Jesse and Jim Millis of High Point, NC. They are low-keyed, selfless, anonymous, Christian and "for-others" kind of charitable persons. They continue to inspire all who know them. The world needs more of this type. I have a feeling that Jesse and Jim would rather I had not placed this in my book. Please excuse me, friends, but I just had to tell it like it is!

In closing this chapter on charities and with full modesty, Susan, my daughter, and I have set up a small family foundation that will grow larger at our deaths. The various trusts and CRT's will ultimately flow into the foundation for others. I'm sorry, Uncle Sam, you are not included! We already have paid you with taxes in the past years.

I can sincerely say that all of my work with charities has been a labor of love. Doing things for others is always satisfying. A warm heart usually is one's only compensation.

There is one side-effect of soliciting charitable contributions. It is very hard to get anyone to go out to dinner with you and your wife. Everyone suspects that it might be a hit for money! We have learned that by telling them up front that this truly is a complete social event, do we receive a positive answer.

In my work with all charities, my energy and drive came from my deep feelings to help others in that so many others had helped me throughout my life. I never sought any rewards for my work in these worthy endeavors. As a by-product of my years of work with The Salvation Army, however, I was honored by receiving their second highest international honor, that being their OTHERS award. Fewer than two dozen of these awards have been given over the past 80-plus years by the High Point Salvation Army. It is an award that I treasure highly and one that tops all the achievements in my lifetime.

CHAPTER 15

Afterthoughts

I have a list of folks I know, all written in a book
And every year at Christmas Time I go and take a look;
And that is when I realize that these names are a part
Not of this book they are written in, but of my very heart.

For each name stands for someone who has crossed my path sometime,
And in that meeting they've become the "Rhythm of Rhyme."
And while it sounds fantastic for me to make this claim,
I really feel that I am composed of EACH AND EVERY NAME.

And while you may not be aware of any special link;
Just meeting you shaped my life more than you think.
For once you've met somebody, the years cannot erase
The memory of a pleasant word or of a friendly face.

So never think my Christmas note is just a mere routine
Of names upon my Christmas list, forgotten in between,
For when I send a Christmas note that is addressed to you
It's because you are on that list of folks that I'm indebted to.

For you are but a total of the many folks I've met
And you happen to be one of those I prefer not to forget.
And whether I have known you for many years or few
In some ways you have had a part in shaping things I do.

And every year when Christmas comes I realize anew
THE BIGGEST GIFT that life can give is MEETING FOLKS
LIKE YOU.

And may the spirit that forever and ever endures
Leave its richest blessings in the heart of you and yours.

THE HAPPIEST OF HOLIDAYS TO YOU.

Author Unknown

Chapter 15 – Afterthoughts

When I started this book, I set out to tell of my simple life. It was not long before I found out that it was not about my life, but rather about all the wonderful people whom I encountered along the way. In untold ways, they all shaped me into what I turned out to be. I suppose most of us have the same conclusion. That is why the verse, that was sent to me years ago, pretty much sums up who I am.

This book is about my journey in pursuit of my dreams. Having dreams is the opposite of being a dreamer! We all have known too many "dreamers." Dreamers dream many dreams but never ever focus on doing anything about them and consequently fail and have miserable lives or failures. Evidently, my dreams impressed me to act upon them. As a result, one can see that these dreams came true for me, at least in time. There are no short cuts to success and never over-night ones! You may have heard the humorous story about a discus thrower: There was a cross-eyed discus thrower who was entered in the Olympic Games. He didn't win any medals, but he sure had the full attention of everyone in the stands. Maybe I am somewhat like that discus thrower and, just maybe, I did catch the attention of a few in the stands during my long career.

As you surely discovered in reading my effort in writing this book, I am neither a scholar nor an accomplished writer. I have tried to write as if I were talking with you in our livingroom. I am a rather informal person and hardly one to "put on airs." I have had fun and joy in my life, wherever it took me, although I realize that my life has been modest compared to some I know. For me, it has been exciting and fulfilling.

The rest of this chapter is made up of afterthoughts and flashbacks of matters which I missed telling about in the prior chapters. I hope they add to the book.

Remembering:

I remember being asked two times by my dear friend, Henry Wilson, just before Christmas, if I would drive the company truck and take him and a truckload of Henredon Furniture samples to the Grandfather Orphanage at Banner Elk for their Christmas. It was an emotional time for Henry and me, as well as for the orphans there. I can still see the excitement on their faces as piece after piece was unloaded. Henry was the giver, but it made Christmas for me and the kids, as they had no warning that Santa Claus was arriving early each of the two years. Henry, in his normal modest way, seemed to be filled with joy. Surprise gifts are the best kind!

Yet another Christmas, I happened to be in Henry Wilson's office about a week before the big day and witnessed him looking out his window as an elderly woman in a house nearby was out in the cold weather scratching to find a lump or two of coal for her stove. Without saying a word, Henry picked up the phone and asked the receptionist to dial the local coal company. He ordered two tons of coal to be delivered promptly to the address next door. He also called a local independent grocery store and told the manager to get up an order of Christmas staples and some extra treats for an elderly widow who lived next to Henredon's office. Both bills were to be sent to him, and he insisted to both merchants that the gifts were to be anonymous. He asked me not to mention this incident. Just the way my friend Henry chose to go through life! Henry carried the true spirit of Christmas in his heart year 'round. And, he bothered to be my friend. Just writing this gives me chills to remember the goodness of Henry Wilson. Can't you imagine what kind of Christmas this elderly lady must have had, even though she never knew from whence it all came? I'm sure she thanked her God for someone who actually cared for her and her needs. Isn't Christmas wonderful when it happens this way?

Occasionally I would, in the course of opening my factory mail, find one of my smallest invoice copies with a note near the bottom of the page, written in the bad handwriting of Henry Wilson, the following: "Thanks! Buy 200 shares of General Electric." I always did and prospered. I believed in that man!

One Christmas Henry Wilson sent beautiful Chatham wool blankets to all of his salesmen's wives as a present. A note attached said, "To keep you warm while your dear husband is traveling!" Needless to say, they were appreciated by all the wives. What a touch of thoughtfulness on Henry's part! This is just another way his mind worked. Every Christmas, Henry obtained from some mountaineer quantities of sour wood honey, had it put in jars that had a label that stated, "This is for your Christmas breakfast — Thanks, Henry." These were sent to all of his salesmen as well as to some key accounts. He was sweetening us up for the year ahead. More than that, he did not forget us. Another small touch of class from a man whom we all loved!

Henry Wilson lived on the telephone. Once, Southern Bell (now Bell South) had a change of managers at the Morganton office, and as the new manager came in and the old one was teaching him the ropes, the new manager said, "Could I possibly meet this man Henry Wilson?" The old manager answered, "Yes, but why?" The new manager said, "Have you looked at his monthly telephone bill?" Henry wanted to stay in touch! At least every second Sunday morning at about 8:45 a.m. I received a telephone call from Henry. That was my time on his schedule. He would usually comment on the orders that I Iemedon received in the past week from me, thank me and then say, "Pistol, you are working too hard!" Then, before he got off the line, he would say, "Pistol, where are you going today?" I usually said to Sunday school and church. He said, "I know that, but where are you going to travel to tonight after you have helped your wife put the babies to bed? If you drove to

A Dream to Sell

Knoxville tonight, you would be the first salesman there Monday morning and be ahead of all the other salesmen all week in the state of Tennessee." This may sound hard, but it was good advice, and Henry knew my favorite time to travel was at night. Most Sunday nights I did leave home after 9 p.m. to travel to distant cities. This is when I had three-and-one-half states. Henry taught us all how to be successful whether we wanted to or not. He was a delight to work for!

Speaking of delight, let me tell you about a delight that our neighborhood boys had growing up. On Friday nights, in summer, we would catch as many lightning bugs as we could and put them in a jar. On Saturday afternoon, we went to the movie theater to see a western movie, taking the jar of lightning bugs with us. After the movie started and the theater was very dark, we would turn the lightning bugs loose at intervals. It was a delight to us, but not necessarily for some of the audience. It is pretty hard to follow a movie with 10 lightning bugs spread out in the dark movie house. We had to make our own excitement in the Great Depression years. I might remind you that movies in those days cost a child only ten cents. We boys usually went at 1 p.m. and stayed until 5, seeing the movie twice on the same dime. We got our money's worth plus much excitement with the bugs that lit up the place. Do kids today have that much fun for ten cents?

At this point, I would like to introduce you to the families of the four founders of Henredon:

Henry Wilson Sr. and Dell Bernhardt Wilson. Three sons, Henry, John and Douglas.

Ralph Edwards. Ralph was a bachelor for many years and later married his secretary at Drexel Furniture, Ruth Harbinson. In their happy marriage they were blessed with two children, Ralph and Betty Hill. Ruth, after the death of her husband in 1957, married James Carr.

Donnell Van Noppen Sr. His wife was Betsy and their two sons are Donnell Jr. and Douglas.

Sterling Collett II. Sterling (the most properly named person I know as to his character) married James Carr's elder sister, Margaret. They have three children, Sterling III, Ruffin ("Dimples") and Martha.

I might add that Margaret Harbinson Hoyle, sister of Ruth Harbinson Edwards Carr, was Henry Wilson's secretary for many years, both at Drexel Furniture and Henredon. She was married to Graham Hoyle who was the assistant superintendent of all manufacturing at Henredon. Graham Hoyle's brother, Carroll "Cac" Hoyle, was in charge of all administration for Henredon from day one of their founding. At the death of Sterling Collett, his brother, John, assumed his position as president of Henredon. As you can see, if you have been able to follow these connections, the Colletts, Edwardses, Carrs, Harbinsons and Hoyles are all intertwined by marriage and very large stockholders of Henredon. It was good to know these connections, if one worked for Henredon.

I must mention the original 12 outstanding salesmen who sold for Henredon. These were professional and very seasoned men whom I joined in 1951. Many other strong salesmen joined us later. For many years, I was known as "the kid" due to my age and inexperience. I learned volumes from these pros. The 12 of us, for the first 20 years, took Henredon's annual sales to approximately $120 million. In my early years there, I would sneak behind partitions and listen, especially, to Jim McGheen, Jack Miller and Steadson Williams as they made their sales pitches to key buyers. I learned from the best of the best. In modesty, I was able in about five years to lead the pack in sales. They all must have been wonderful teachers!

I had had several ponies when I was growing up, but never a horse. It was in about 1965 that I bought two horses from my uncle, Harry

Wilson. Uncle Harry had had these horses for his two granddaughters, "Cookie" (Elizabeth) and "Candy" (Susan) Wilson. One of the horses was named Katie and she was a fantastic Morgan. The other one was just a horse, and I soon sold him. The granddaughters met boys, and horses then dropped way down the list of things to do. That was how I was able to make a real deal with my uncle. Katie was a real pleasure to own and ride. She was gaited and could jump as well. We later added two other American saddle-bred horses, Lady and Rex. They were high steppers and very smooth to ride. Lady was trained to pull a buggy, so we bought an antique buggy, and I was able to get the craftsman at Schoonbeck Furniture in their off-hours to completely refurbish it with red leather seats and all. We painted the buggy yellow and fine-striped the wheels in red. What fun we did have with it especially at Gingercake. Horses afforded our entire family fun and joy for over 25 years. I even learned to shoe them! We kept our horses with Mr. and Mrs. K.F. Green near Willow Creek in High Point in the winter and, of course, trailered them to Gingercake for the summer. One learns something special by owning a horse and developing a bond with them. I sold the horses in about 1988, much to my later regret. I may yet get back into the horse business!

In this book I have written much about Gingercake, our summer home, and how much fun we've had there for over 52 years. Well, I think it's time for me to introduce our great neighbors there: Rosemary and Raymond Stamey (caretaker); Pam and Ed McClure (mowing) and Charles ("Tuna") and Nancy Maxwell (water superintendent). It is special to have neighbors who care for one another. All three of our above-mentioned neighbors live at Gingercake year-around. I would also like to recall the late Arlee Barrier, who was our dear friend and who could do anything you wanted done to your home. He died several years ago to the sorrow of all. Arlee could pour foundations, lay blocks and bricks, do master carpentering, electrical work and plumbing, paint, wallpaper and lay carpet. He could do it all. What a friend to have!

If you are ready for a tall fish story, I have one that is connected to my father. Daddy and Mother's summer cottage at Gingercake was located across Upper Creek from our home there. Their cottage was not on the creek, so Daddy decided to dig a small trout pond in his front yard. He spent much time, effort, and money on this project and stocked it full of beautiful rainbow trout. In the winter months of January, February and March they would come to High Point and occupy an apartment that we had built for them in our home. One February, Daddy received a telephone call from "Newt" Clark who ran a small country store near Gingercake. Newt reported the bad news that there had been an automobile accident in front of Dad's home and the gas and oil had run into his trout pond and all 35 of his beautiful rainbow trout were floating on top, dead. Dad was heart-broken and very mad. I tried to calm him down by telling him that we would restock the pond in the spring and for him not to be concerned. This was of no comfort to him. He made several telephone calls to Gingercake in an effort to determine who the person was who owned the auto in the wreck and his insurance company. After much pleading on my part for him not to file an insurance claim for the death of 35 fish, he did it anyway. By coincidence, the insurance adjuster was a childhood friend of mine who lived in Lenoir. When he called my dad, I answered the telephone. I told "Flea" that I had tried to talk my dad out of filing the claim for the fish killed in an auto wreck, but to no avail. I added that it would be a strange entry for his insurance company to understand. Flea insisted that there would not be a problem, and he went on to say that he needed to know how big the trout were and what was the value of each. I told my friend that I knew the fishing places in the mountains that let you fish there and they charged three dollars a pound for one's catch. I explained to him the

35 rainbows averaged about three pounds. Flea said that would be a total of $315, and the check would be in the mail shortly. When I reported this to Daddy, he was all smiles. His persistence had paid off, regardless of the strange claim. He would be back in the trout business in the spring. Maybe, just maybe, some of his persistent genes had been passed on to his son. A professional salesman needs an abundance of persistence!

Dave Parmelee worked at Henredon as an assistant to the great Kenneth Volz, master furniture designer. One day, Dave needed a ride at lunchtime to downtown Morganton and asked Sterling Collett, vice president at Henredon, for a ride. I must tell you about all cars owned by Sterling. He never had them washed or vacuumed out on the inside. He smoked, and the ashtrays were always overflowing. Obviously this was not a priority for Sterling. Of course, Sterling said that he would be delighted to take Dave downtown. On entering the car, Dave took a look at the interior of the auto and jumped back and muttered, "Sterling, this is a slum on wheels!" Typical of Sterling, he simply smiled and cranked his car for the trip downtown for these two opposite characters. They were both Harvard men. I have always heard that you could tell a Harvard man, but not much.

I think it's time to laugh a little. I would like to explain a humorous thing that happened to me on the return trip in 1978, from China. We stopped over in Paris, France, to rest before we returned home. The month was January, and snow had fallen the night before, and in fact it was still snowing when we visited the Palace at Versailles and also the Great Cathedral at Chartres (the most beautiful stained glass windows in the world). Naturally, we were all bundled up in winter clothes. I fell in behind one of the ladies on our trip to hike about a half mile to the famous cathedral. I suddenly realized that with each step she took, she was walking her snow slacks off by stepping on them. She was a good sport when I told her what was happening to her, albeit a little embarrassed. We found a park bench, and I helped to pull up her pants. We all had hearty laughs. I may be the only man in history who helped a lady in Paris to put on her pants! Please forgive me, that was a naughty remark, but it happened!

Speaking of Paris, I have yet another most unusual story. You remember Betty Culler Jackson, Rhett Jackson's wife, and Kathleen Culler, Betty's mother, from South Carolina. Well, Betty and Kathleen were on a tour of France and found themselves at the top of the Eiffel Tower in Paris. While they were enjoying the scenery and using their very southern accents to communicate, some gentleman walked up to them and introduced himself and his wife, saying they were the C.T. Ingrams from High Point, North Carolina. The Ingrams knew these ladies had to be from the South, and after a week or so of hearing nothing but French, they were delighted to meet someone who spoke their language. Betty Jackson said instantly, "Do you all know Plato Wilson in High Point?" Of course, C.T. said that they did. What a small world this is! It was nice, for me, to learn later that my name had been mentioned in high places (390 feet high). What a coincidence.

One of the most fun things I did in my career was at Christmas time. I purchased a real Santa Claus suit and visited all my business clients in a 50-mile driving distance of High Point. I passed out "candy kisses" and insisted that they all should be "good little children" if they wanted me to treat them well on Christmas morning. I did this for 30 years before I retired and still do it in my 12 years of retirement. I even was invited to my dealers' Christmas parties to hand out treats. Everybody believes in Santa Claus at Christmas time! Occasionally I would forget an account and not visit the store on my holiday rounds. You can be assured that I received telephone calls to find out the time of my visit. You cannot believe the fun I had doing this annual visiting. I never was aware of any salesman in the business who took the time to establish this good will. Sometimes I visited the offices of other furniture manufacturers who were competitors. I suppose it takes someone with a little show biz in their soul to bring this off. I have come a very long way from my introverted days of being 12 and 13 years of age. My wife Dixie joins me in her own Santa Claus attire, and we visit friends during the Christmas season, often bearing gifts.

Truisms Remembered:

• *Success is doing all the little things that an ordinary person chooses not to do.* I included this truism on my stationery at the bottom for my entire business career. It is not only true, but was a constant reminder to me for what I was to do each and every day. It works!

• *Success is not a worldly gain, but the life we live each day.* This was the motto for our class of '43 at Morganton High School. What a great thought to carry into the world and to think about for our lifetime. I found it to be true!

• *"The only reason to be a salesman is to know your customers, to satisfy them and service them."* — Carl Levine, the famous merchant of Bloomingdale's New York City: That very distilled definition speaks in volumes. A goal to achieve! I cannot improve on this advice.

• *Being organized is the best way to succeed.* How often have we seen brilliant people, who were not organized, fail? Being organized, well informed, with passion, allows one to communicate one's position on matters that are important. Being organized in one's time allows one to be very productive. Not being organized is a blueprint for failure.

• *The three W's — wine, women and wives.* Drinking to excess, chasing women and having wives who will not allow husbands to travel their territories properly are the most prevalent reasons many well-prepared and competent traveling salesmen fail. I have witnessed this too often in my professional career. It is a tragedy. One may be surprised that I include wives. Unfortunately, this happens too often.

• *Shirt sleeves to shirt sleeves in three generations.* I heard my father and his friends say this so often as I grew up. It was a while before I learned what this truism is all about. It was their way of saying, from their observations and experience, that one generation makes it, the next spends it and the third has to start all over again. From my position as a child of the depression era of the 1930s, I had a hard time adjusting to this. I thought that if a family was to be successful financially that family should feel blessed and would certainly preserve their way of life. Later, I too observed that the fortune reversal was truly the final outcome in too many cases. If one were to bet on this happening, one would win 85 percent of the time. How unfortunate! Surely we can do better, but the lack of motivation by later generations comes into play.

• *Where you find great pools of money, you often find crooks.* As I sit writing this book and witnessing the corporate scandals abounding in our great nation and even in high-sounding charities, I value this truism. We all have heard too much in the past of union bosses and the Mafia swarming around pools of money and are tempted to have sticky hands. So, I suppose someone who fashioned this truism had it right. Where have the morals gone?

• *Indispensability.* My mother was a great teacher in spite of her limited education. She was very loving and caring, street smart, observing, hard-working, and most of all she possessed a head full of common sense. There is no doubt that she had more influence in my life than any other person. She instilled in me the possibility that I could be whatever I chose to be. Mother also taught me the other side of success: Never should one believe he or she was indispensable. She used the following story to teach the lesson: She suggested that I put my fist into a bucket of water and then pull it out to see if it left a hole in the water. Of course the answer was that no one was indispensable!

A Dream to Sell

A very marvelous lesson for all of us who might, at some point in our lives, think that we are "the cock of the walk."

- *If you don't use it, you lose it.* This truism is easy to understand and generally accepted by all. However, putting it into practice is another matter. Too many get compliant and lazy and rest on their laurels without staying engaged in contemporary events. I was always in the environment of younger people as I progressed in my selling career. They never let me relax and become disengaged. I think this is why I have remained young at heart. Staying engaged is true in every phase of our lives: keeping our bodies in shape by diet and exercise, our social life, our work life, our religious life, and yes, our sex life. A lifetime is a journey, and that journey is as good as we make it.

- *The essence of charity.* The story that follows may explain my deep-seated philosophy on charity: There was a very successful fishing boat captain who, upon returning to the dock, noticed a disheveled looking man on the dock. That man approached the fishing captain and asked for a couple of fish to feed his family. The captain gave him the fish, gladly. The next day the same thing happened, and the captain again tossed him some fish. The beggar was on the dock the third day, with outstretched hands. The captain said to him, "Mister, I think that I should give you a fishhook and some line, and I will teach you how to fish for yourself from the dock." The moral of this story is obvious: Give a man a fish and he will ask for more; teach him how to fish for himself and he will be self-sufficient. Most of the people in need would rather have someone take the time to teach them how to be self-sufficient than to beg. This moral has been proven to me many times in my extensive work with the Salvation Army. They show compassion but also take the time to teach.

- *"Perhaps the most valuable result of all education is the ability to make yourself do the things you have to do when it has to be done, whether you like it or not."* — Thomas Huxley, Englishman. Discipline is another word for this. Disciplined habits are the hardest of all to develop, for we all are guilty of just putting it off until tomorrow, especially the tough problems. If one gives in to this procrastination, it tends to over-flow into all phases of one's life. A disciplined life is a thing of beauty and an inspiration to others.

• *The most powerful force on earth is a human soul on fire.* This is also known as "passion for your mission." Without passion, nothing is accomplished. This truism worked for me.

• *If a person is content with what he or she has done, he will never become great for what he will do.* Never become complacent. It is a dead-ly disease! He who stops being better stops being good, is another way to explain this truism.

• *A professional salesman is a teacher.* Teaching is the way to con-vert others to a better idea. Successful teaching enlarges the army to accomplish much. One alone can only accomplish so much.

• *Salesmanship is the lubricant of commerce.* Without the sale, nobody works.

• *Genius, that power which dazzles mortal eyes, is often perseverance in disguise.* Enough said!

• *"It's not the ship so much as the skillful sailing that assures the pros-perous voyage."* — George Curtis. I do believe that George got this right.

• *Four untrainable traits from Eastman Kodak.* This dynamic nation-al firm, in analyzing its sales training program, found four traits that were possibly untrainable:

    1. To be a self-starter;

    2. To have job commitment;

    3. To be persistent, and

    4. To possess initiative.

These vital traits must be within the individual from the begin-ning. Without these traits, one cannot go very far in any endeavor. A very strong desire to succeed and passion can help develop these vital traits.

• *There are ways to overcome recessions*. The next story should help one more fully understand one aspect of a recession and how to deal with this problem which occurs from time to time:

"THE HOTDOG STORY"

A man lived by the side of the road and sold hotdogs.

He was hard of hearing so he had no radio.

He had trouble with his eyes so he read no newspapers.

But he sold good hotdogs.

He put a sign on the highway telling how good they were.

He stood by the side of the road and cried, "Buy a hotdog, Mister."

And people bought.

He increased his meat and roll orders.

He bought a bigger stove to take care of his trade.

He got his son home from college to help him.

But then something happened...

His son said, "Father, haven't you been listening to the radio?

If money stays 'tight,' we are bound to have bad business.

There may be a big depression coming on.

You had better prepare for poor trade."

Whereon the father thought, "Well, my son has been to college.

He reads the papers and he listens to the radio, and he ought to know."

So the father cut down on his meat and roll orders.

Took down his advertising signs.

And no longer bothered to stand on the highway to sell hotdogs.

And his hotdog sales fell almost overnight.

"You're right, son," the father said to the boy.

"We are certainly headed for a depression."

Author Unknown

A Dream to Sell

During my 44 years of selling, my dealers and I lived through eight recessions. They were not fun. Each time we had one, I would write my accounts pep rally letters and attach the "hotdog" story, lest they forget that the best medicine for a recession is a positive mental attitude. The news media always overdid their coverage. It is best to just tune them out!

• *Motivation is when our dreams put on work clothes.* In this book, I have written much about dreams and dreamers. The difference is that people who dream and want to succeed do what the above truism states: They put on their work clothes and make it happen. Dreamers, however, do not have work clothes, so they think only "how it could be" and dream on!

• *"Not in the clamor of the crowded street, not in the shouts and plaudits of the throng, but in ourselves are triumph and defeat."* — Henry Wadsworth Longfellow. This is, by far, my favorite truism of all times. It is the answer to the "blame game" alibi. It squarely puts the responsibility of any endeavor on the individual in charge. Now we know. This truism has traveled with me every day of my life.

What are the most important values that I learned in my long life? I learned to have a vision always, be passionate in all undertakings, learn to deal with constant change, be flexible, always have hope and faith, and a leader must be able to inspire others.

After this heavy reading, you might enjoy a funny story from my childhood as I grew up in Morganton, located in Burke County. In past years, Burke County was known for humorous real life character who lived there. My former neighbor Senator Sam Ervin II was an example of one, albeit a scholarly one. This story is set in the little town about 10 miles west of Morganton, Glen Alpine. The town had two very prominent families, the Pittses and the Gileses. They were in business together. All traffic going west in North Carolina traveled on Highway 70 that went through the middle of Glen Alpine. One Sunday, at approximately 10:45 a.m., a tourist realized that his gas tank was almost empty and at the same time he spotted a rundown service station that had two of those old-fashioned-type hand-pump dispensers. He realized that all gas stations in those days closed for Sunday church services at 11:00 a.m., but he pulled into the station and a sleepy looking old mountaineer came out. The tourist asked if he could possibly obtain a tank of gas before his station closed for church. The sleepy looking man said that he could. During this time, the tourist, impressed with the beauty of this village, asked the attendant if God had a church in this village. The mountaineer removed his hat and scratched his head and said, "Mister, all that I know is that Mr. Pitts has a church on that yonder hill and Mr. Giles has one over there on the other hill. I'm not sure if God has a church here." Well, we all have known churches that have been dominated by individuals.

HUMOROUS SALES CALLS

I think one of the most humorous — and tragic — sales calls I ever made was the one I made on Whitley Furniture Company in Zebulon, NC, back in the 1950s. I represented Heritage-Henredon Furniture at the time. I had made many tries in an effort to open this fine account. At the time, Whitley was one of those combination funeral homes and furniture stores cited earlier in this book. The managers of this combination were Mr. and Mrs. Screws. I had been led to believe that on my next call they would give me that opening order. I was there to do just that. I was well prepared and made a mighty sales pitch to them. Over the two hours of doing this and selecting the proper pieces to be ordered, the telephone rang and Mr. Screws went to answer it. Mrs. Screws and I sat waiting. Shortly, we heard the raised voice of Mr. Screws into the telephone, "Don't do it, I want to come out and speak with you first!" We later learned that some dejected farmer with a failed crop of tobacco had told Mr. Screws that he was going to commit suicide right then and that he wanted Mr. Screws to come and pick up his body. That explained the loud voice we had heard. Mr. Screws subsequently told us that he heard a pistol shot before he could hang up the phone. He departed the store immediately and left Mrs. Screws and me without the confirmation to order the merchandise as he was the only one who could grant an order. I packed up my sales material with double sorrow, sad for the unfortunate farmer and sad also for coming so close to obtaining that long-awaited opening order. No doubt, I had been "screwed" out of that order! Later, the account was opened successfully.

Back in the '50s I had helped one of Mecklenburg Furniture Shops' renowned interior designers, by the name of "Choat," to select furnishings for a fabulous summer home in Blowing Rock. He was ordering some of my furniture as well as items from other very fine lines. I did not know Choat too well other than that he was a great designer. When all the furnishings arrived and the carpet and draperies were ready to be installed, Choat disappeared and went on an extended drunk. Ralph Short, the son of the owner of Mecklenburg Furniture Shops, was assigned to install the job. Well, Ralph had no idea as to the placement of the furnishings, draperies or carpet. No drawings could be found. So off to Blowing Rock Ralph went, with the trucks full of all the furnishings. Going by the paint colors and the sizes of the rooms, he slowly installed the draperies and carpet. Placement of some of the furniture was obvious. The sofas and chairs, occasional furniture and accessories, however, remained an unknown. Ralph ran me down by telephone to see if I could help him on these mysteries. I could help him some but not entirely. He called other factory salesmen for the same help with furniture bought from them. It was a nightmare! The problem with Choat and other similar designers, as I witnessed in my selling experience, was that they simply got cold feet on big installations, wondering if everything would fit and look proper. They could not face reality, so they resorted to putting on a disappearing act to escape. Choat was so good with customers that the Shorts took him back in after this episode, albeit with much lecturing and many promises made.

Late one afternoon, after having completed a call on Fowler Brothers in Knoxville, I proceeded to check out of the Farragut Hotel to travel to the historic town of Greenville, TN. This is the town that the future vice president to Abraham Lincoln and then President of the United States Andrew Johnson had his tailoring business, located on the town square. Most of the buildings there were old and of yesteryear. The first bad omen I encountered was that the bellhop at the Farragut put my suitcase in a car going west to Nashville and put another bag in my car going northeast to Greenville. I did not notice this error until I was checking into the Greenville Hotel, which had to be over 100 years old. I immediately called the Farragut and reported the error. As it turned out, the man going west had already discovered the mixup and had left my bag at the Farragut. We each were to place the wrong bags on buses for overnight delivery to Nashville and Greenville. Mine arrived at about nine o'clock that evening. That episode was just the beginning! The next alarm went off when the desk clerk issued me a chamber pot and told me that the master toilet was down my hallway. This was a new wrinkle in my experience in traveling. There I was with no suitcase and no private bath. On entering my assigned room, I flipped on the light switch to find one small light suspended from the ceiling. That was it! Then I noticed something coiled up in the corner of the semi-dark room. My first thought was that it might be a snake. Later, cautiously, I found that the "coil" was actually a large rope with a neat sign that said, "In case of fire, throw one end of this rope out the window for your escape." Well, things were going from bad to worse! At nine o'clock, I was delighted when the bus arrived at the bus station and I was able to take my bag back to my shabby room. I went to sleep wondering who would wake me up in case of a fire. As to the chamber pot, I didn't have to use it because this was long before I learned anything about prostate glands. I made it through the night and was able to call on my friend Bill Doughty and receive a small order. As I departed Greenville, I asked myself, "Was this trip really necessary?" Nothing about it was humor-ous to me at the time, but in later years it became an unusual memory to reflect upon. No one ever said that life on the road was easy!

My final story is about a call I made on Jones Brothers' Furniture in Smithfield, NC. The occasion was one of the store's giant January once-a-year clearance sales. On these occasions, the Jones brothers would invite all of their major-brand sales agents to come and help them out with the huge crowds. The event had all the atmosphere of a county fair, with the brothers serving barbecue at dinner to all invit-ed salesmen. At the close of the day, we went to eat that marvelous meal. It was during the night that the store caught fire and burned to the ground. Most salesmen had left their travel cases in the store upon leaving the night before. That left them in a very bad way. I was not one of those unfortunates. The huge warehouses were not attached to the store, so they escaped the fire. Bright and early the next day, the brothers — and the rest of us — met in the warehouses to resume business. The phone rang, and one of the brothers answered it to hear an elderly man's voice say, "I heard about your fire. I was in your store yesterday afternoon and I inadvertently left my hat on a dining room table there. Have you found it?" Of course, the Jones brothers had lost the store and all of its contents, and here was a man worrying about a 20-dollar hat! The brother on the other end of the phone simply said they would look for it, but they suspected it was burned in the big fire. But this is not the end of the story. Some months later, on one of my routine visits to Smithfield, as I was waiting my turn to see the buyer, I noticed this dapper gentleman walk up and ask to see the owner in regards to their recent fire. He was the insurance adjuster with a huge check to present to the Joneses for their fire claim. Someone spoke up and said that he should see "Smokie," one of the brothers. With the mention of Smokie, the adjuster's face turned a variety of colors! The claim was legitimate, and the brothers were paid, but not before the adjuster had second thoughts and the rest of us had hearty laughs. I have found that most humor is the result of some tragedy. So, the Jones brothers' fire was a tragedy that turned out later to cause some hearty laughter.

CONCLUSION:

Alfred Lord Tennyson on the character Ulysses (The Roman name for Odysseus, in Greek mythology, the hero of the Trojan War who spent ten years returning home): "I am a part of all that I have met." My life cannot be compared to the great Ulysses, but the end quote is the same. Were it not for the remarkable people whom I was privileged to know and learn from, my life would have been much less than it is. In a lot of my life, and especially in retirement since 1990, I have tried to thank those past friends for their gifts to me. I have used my work with charities to accomplish this end. Of course, one cannot actually thank all of those of the past because death has taken its share, but one can thank the many others who are currently coming up the ladder. I wish and urge others to do the same!

Appendix

And in those days, behold, there came through the gates of the city a salesman from afar off, and it came to pass as the day went by he sold plenty.

And in that city were they that were the order takers and they that spent their days in adding to the alibi sheets. Mightily were they astonished. They said one to the other, "How doth he getteth away with it?" And it came to pass that many were gathered in the back office and a soothsayer came among them. And he was one wise guy. And they spoke and questioned him saying, "How is it that this stranger accomplisheth the impossible?"

Whereupon the soothsayer made answer. "He of whom you speak is one hustler. He ariseth very early in the morning and goeth forth full of pep. He complaineth not, neither doth he know despair. He is arrayed in purple and fine linen, while ye go forth with pants unpressed.

"While ye gather here and say one to the other, 'Verily this is a terrible day to work,' he is already abroad. And when the eleventh hour cometh, he needeth no alibis. He knoweth his line and they that would stave him off, they give him orders. Men say unto him 'nay' when he cometh in, yet when he goeth forth he hath their names on the line that is dotted.

"He taketh with him the two angels 'inspiration' and 'perspiration' and worketh to beat hell. Verily I say unto you, go and do likewise."

Author Unknown

Henredon
fine furniture

PLATO S. WILSON
January 21, 1981
STATE OF THE TERRITORY

Election years seem to be tough years for business! We have just finished such a year: Inflation, a tampered economy, high interest rates, and the "bad" dredged to the top. In spite of these facts, 1980 was an excellent year for us in the quality furniture business! You did an <u>outstanding job</u> for yourselves and Henredon. This makes your progress even more appreciated. <u>You are professionals!</u> I take great pride in bragging on each of you. You have once again made me appear as a good salesman. Oliver Cromwell once said, "He who stops being better stops being good!" This is a challenge!

1981 will be a challenge! We hear too much "doom and gloom" around. We've heard this before! Let's look a little deeper than the media. 1981 is a turnaround year — the start of new growth. We have a very popular new president who wants to help business! The first quarter will be competitive but not bad for us in the Southeast and in the quality business that we are in. There is money at the top! We are in a growth business! One mighty important thing to remember — there will be a tax cut and this money could come to us in the furniture business. Interest rates and inflation will drop this year. These are good signs. Believe me, we will record 1981 as a very good year if we <u>keep ourselves optimistic.</u> <u>Remember:</u> "A pessimist is one who makes difficulties of his opportunities; an optimist is one who makes opportunities of his difficulties." With this in mind, let's face 1981 <u>optimistically</u>!

<u>"Man"</u> is the principal syllable in <u>management</u>! You can see I am getting around to the key word for 1981 — <u>management</u>! A man who follows the crowd will never be followed by a crowd! The best leaders are those most interested in surrounding themselves with assistants and associates smarter than they are — being frank in admitting this — and willing to pay for such talent! Good morale in any organization is faith in the man at the top. I am giving management a lot of credit, but some of it is qualified. Are you that kind of management? I'm sure you are good, but you can be better! Your

actions are <u>observed</u>, <u>studied</u>, <u>criticized</u> and <u>praised</u>. You are important to the welfare of many. Have you had the time to think and plan your business the way that it ought to be? Are you always optimistic as is necessary? Do you stick to your charter of progress? Do you motivate your people and customers? Are you aware that the difference between failure and success is doing a thing nearly right and doing it exactly right? Management is the starting point of success! <u>That's you!</u> My only plan in this letter is to stress the importance of the man at the top. The quality of his work is spoken in the people beneath him. You have great and rewarding <u>responsibilities</u> — you are the "sparkplug" of your company. Do your job well in 1981, and you will make money! For you will appraise your daily operation, select great personnel, buy the best products (Henredon) and inspire your people to make more money for themselves. I have faith that you will be and do all these things starting now — <u>for I know you well and have great confidence in you</u>. I am in somewhat the same circumstance. I have the same responsibilities as you for leadership in 1981; I must do all the things I've reminded you to do. <u>Together</u> we will take our bow as this great year is accomplished. My great and honored former nextdoor neighbor, Senator Sam Ervin, quotes <u>his</u> old school teacher: "The world is a grindstone — whether you let it grind you down or polish you up, depends on you!" This is exactly the way I see it, also! I like polish better, don't you? Let us <u>all</u> show our best in 1981 and do it better than ever. You can count on my dedication and help — <u>every day</u> of this grand year that is ours. Thank goodness for our great partner — <u>Henredon</u> which will be a tool in our hands. "If anything will sell, Henredon will sell!"

Please review your sales figures below. Several of you call them your "report cards." Whatever you call them, they are very important to me and Henredon. Thank you very much for your tremendous effort — past and future!

Motivated,

Plato S. Wilson

	1978	1979	1980
Wood			
Upholstery			
Total			

PLATO S. WILSON

January 28, 1982

STATE OF THE TERRITORY MESSAGE

"The grass must bend when the wind blows across it." (Confucius 500 B.C.) He could have said the same thing in 1981 had he been around. I don't believe any of us have seen so much turbulence as we saw during this windy year. However, as Confucius said — to survive, we had to be flexible — and we were! Most all of us bent when it was necessary and have come back strong as a result. Now we know what game it is that we are playing. We have to <u>return</u> to being <u>excellent</u> <u>merchants</u>! It is an ill wind that blows no good!

The exciting thing now is 1982! I will assure you, now, that you will record 1982 as a good year if we return to the basics and be the expert merchants we must be. A man who is content with what he has done will never become great for what <u>he</u> <u>will</u> <u>do</u>! 1982 is going to be the most interesting and rewarding year you will witness for some time. The famous Charles F. Kettering said, "We work day after day, not to finish things, but to make the future better...because we will spend the rest of our lives there!"

I think the key word for 1982 will be <u>hard</u> <u>work</u>! I've had fun with that word all my life. I have a theory that you must work hard all the time! In good times to get all the business, and in bad times to get enough! I hope you share this theory. The world owes us nothing — it was here first!

As you know, inflation is abating, interest rates are falling, the economy has had much medicine. Now for the cure! A forward-looking merchant will adjust his business as to expenses and begin again to build a profes-

sional staff. He will have to train his sales people in the basics of good man-
ners, good spirit, extra service (not just service), and be a real sparkplug to
them. Leadership must start at the top. Dwight D. Eisenhower's philosophy
was: "I believe when you are in any contest you should work like there is,
to the last minute, a chance to lose it!" With this dedicated attitude, you
will win. When Alexander the Great was asked how he conquered the
world, he replied — "By not delaying." So let's get on with this exciting
year of 1982.

I think that I can help you by motivating your staff and giving them the
needed sales information that they will require to make the sale of my
product HENKEL-HARRIS. I feel like a 21-year-old and have the
enthusiasm to go with this age — so watch out! I personally believe 1982
will be excellent and I will help you make it a fact. When you go fishing,
you take your best equipment and the best of all baits. You don't just use
any old line and any old bait. With HENKEL-HARRIS you will have the
best line possible to make that profitable sale because I am convinced it
is the best of its type, and now <u>our</u> <u>service</u> is also the best. With the addition of our <u>solid</u> <u>Walnut</u> <u>line</u> to go with the Cherry and Mahogany, we
have a world beater. Attach all of this to your new dedication of being
the best merchant in your region and with my constant help — we will
do what is necessary to make you proud of 1982! I sincerely mean this! I
can hardly wait to get started. How about you?

As I close these remarks, I would like to leave you with this challenging
quote from the great Englishman — Thomas Huxley: "Perhaps the most
valuable result of all education is the ability to make yourself do the thing
you have to do, when it has to be done, whether you like it or not."

Very excited,

Plato S. Wilson

Success is – doing all the little things that an ordinary person chooses not to do!

PLATO S. WILSON

January 26, 1985

STATE OF THE TERRITORY MESSAGE

There is an old Persian proverb that goes like this: "Thinking well is wise; planning well is wiser; doing well, wisest and best of all!" I can see clearly that you did "*think*," "*plan*," and most of all "*did*" exceedingly well for Henkel-Harris in 1984! For you gave us a +31% increase in sales for our territory! How sweet it is! And in the doing, I sincerely hope you helped yourself — the most important accomplishment of all! Thank you!

1985 is *another* of those rare vintage years that offers us another "beautiful rose" — ours for the plucking! But, we will have to "*position*" ourselves to take advantage of this enormous reward! Being the *best* and most *professional* merchant in your area will be number one in your plan. We will have to continue to *train* and *motivate* your sales staff to be at top performance. A *satisfied customer* still is our best advertisement! For, *they will tell others*! Also, when no new thoughts fill our minds — when no new horizons beckon — when life is in the past, not in the future, we are on the way to *uselessness*! Or, maybe it's like the old adage: "I can complain because rose bushes have thorns *or* rejoice because thorn bushes have roses — it's all in how you look at it!" What the future holds for us depends on what we hold for the future. Hard working "todays" make high winning "tomorrows"! Here I go with another "sugar message" about the year ahead. I must tell you "like it is" — otherwise, I would not merit your partnership for 1985!

The really key word for 1985 for *Henkel-Harris* stores will be anticipation! To improve your stock turn and profit, we will have to continue to "plan ahead" from future cuttings. This will make your selling much easier and insure a fan-

---

tastic year! Our buyers buy a lot of Henkel-Harris but never have much stock to sell. Bear with my recommendation this year and we will do very well. The risk factor will be very, very low! For everyone would really like to own Henkel-Harris if you will allow them to do so by having *stock* of this *best quality line*. Let us not forget these positive facts: (1) the economy will stay strong, (2) housing starts at a record height, (3) interest rates declining, (4) Reagan is in the White House, (5) war babies are 35-40 years old with much money to spend and buying traditional furniture, and (6) Henkel-Harris turns "lookers" into "buyers"! A store that owns Henkel-Harris stock has "money in the bank"! So, let's get busy buying this great product for fall deliveries! *Do not cancel a single piece*. If you ever have the thought, contact me and I will relieve you of any stock! Our rice carved bed is still the *best bed in the nation* and also the best selling one!

In addition to the key word *anticipation*, *optimism* ranks with it! As this word will be a great part of our "state of mind" in 1985, let me define this word: "optimism is getting married at 90 and looking for a house near a school!" Since we are not that old, our job should be much easier!

Thank you, again, for your loyalty, patience and courtesies you have shown to me over the years. I would like to leave this excellent thought with you for 1985: "It's not the ship so much as the skillful sailing that assures the prosperous voyage!" (George Curtis)

As is my custom, I am listing below three-year sales patterns for your firm. I know these figures reflect much good planning, hard selling and support of your many fine employees. We at Henkel-Harris do sincerely appreciate all of this effort. May the fragrant smell of the rose be with you throughout 1985. A friend is a present you give yourself — I would like to be that present!

Optimistically,

Plato S. Wilson

1982	1983	1984

HENKEL-HARRIS®

COMPANY, INCORPORATED
Manufacturers of Fine Furniture

PLATO S. WILSON
January 21, 1989
STATE OF THE TERRITORY

There was this very proper New Englander who was invited to visit his "new, rich" Texas friend. The Texan, with his ten gallon hat and boots, took his guest on a tour in his jeep of his vast wasteland spread — tumble-weeds and all. While touring a bird flew up and the guest asked what kind of bird that was. "A bird of paradise," came the reply! The guest simply said, "He sure is a long way from home!" That bird's home had to be in our territory — a paradise in many ways! In spite of an election year, you did for us a tremendous job in 1988 — allowing me a 9% increase. "The rung of a ladder was never meant to rest upon, but only to hold a man's foot long enough to enable him to put the other somewhat higher." (Thomas Huxley)

Let's talk about the last year of this decade — 1989! From all I can read of the research available, I conclude 1989 will be excellent for our territory. The vital signs still look very good; the Fed slowed down the economy in mid '88 to save us from inflation and problems ahead; interest rates are still decent; record low unemployment; the Bush administration will address, successfully, the two deficits. He is the best prepared President we've had in many years! Don't sell him short!

The key word for 1989 should be *"perspective"*! There has been more change in the furniture industry in the last couple of years than all of my forty years. Not all good. The trend by the *Power Factories* is to take your business away from you with very harsh demands. This is wrong and will not work! There is no substitute for good old everyday selling and an exchange of ideas between buyer and seller. Power plays do not succeed! After all, it's *your money and gamble*. All of this is going to only enhance a line as Henkel-Harris. We are old fashioned and let you tell *us* how you want to run your business. We just simply supply you with America's best product to sell, and we service your needs! Truly, there are not many quality casegoods lines that have this policy. We will just get bigger and better with you, I'm sure you agree. The *Power Factories* have made a bad mistake; they have put all of "their eggs in too few baskets"! This is a violation of basic sales principles. They are turning their backs on a lot of *good*, *strong* and *capable* merchants. We love all of you and simply want to be a part of your success. Thank you for being our friend in the past and the future!

As you know, no stock orders have been taken by Henkel-Harris in the last twelve months. As a result, we have reduced our backlog of orders by one year. This should be good news to you. When we stopped booking orders (Feb. '88), our deliveries were into August/September '89. We are still there! Henkel-Harris has indicated to me that it will be late spring or summer before they will again let us book stock orders — with possibly a price increase prior to that time! They are going to make it more difficult to obtain our product. Some kind of quota will be used so as not to repeat our past backlog. Please study this very carefully as you review your present backlog of orders. I truly believe that you and I maximized our earlier projections that made you a lot of profit and sold a lot of furniture. We've learned that anticipation is correct! I hope you agree that I have helped you during this past year. I am impressed with *your courage*, *your ability* and *your confidence* in Henkel-Harris! You *bought*, *paid for* and *sold* a massive amount of our product. You see, with encouragement, you can rise to the occasion. You remind me of what Henry Austin had to say, "Genius, that power which dazzles mortal eyes, is often perseverance in disguise"!

I believe that 1989, the beginning of the eighth consecutive year of growth in the U.S. economy, will be a "*workplace*" for us to display our *abilities* and *expertise*. If you don't use your skills, you lose them! I hope you, again, welcome me as your partner, and we will produce good work together. We don't want it ever said of you and me: "They used to be good." As we approach 1989, let us think about a very famous quote by Henry Wadsworth Longfellow: "Not in the clamor of the crowded street, not in the shouts and plaudits of the throng, but in ourselves are triumph and defeat." Let us be *confident*, *alert* and *very optimistic* as we make this year, by far, our best year with the help of all the good people at Henkel-Harris! It's going to be fun!

Just look at what *you have done* in three very exciting years! A pretty good "*Report Card*"! Good luck and a **MOST HAPPY AND PROSPEROUS NEW YEAR!**

Most Sincerely,

Plato S. Wilson (Grateful)

1986	1987	1988
_____	_____	_____

CAREER SALES: PLATO S. WILSON

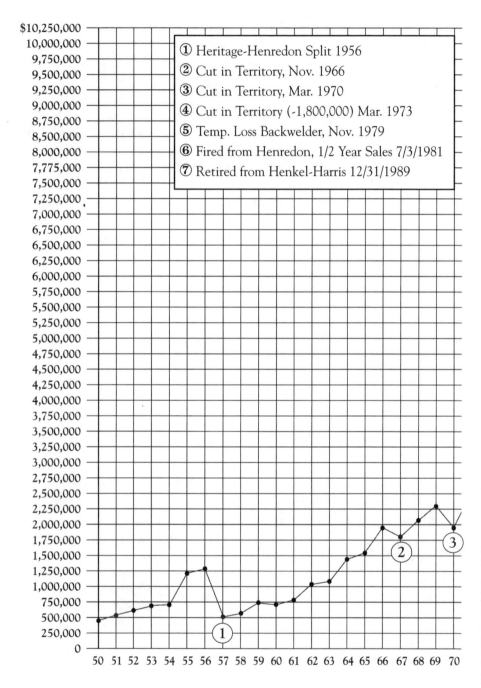

① Heritage-Henredon Split 1956
② Cut in Territory, Nov. 1966
③ Cut in Territory, Mar. 1970
④ Cut in Territory (-1,800,000) Mar. 1973
⑤ Temp. Loss Backwelder, Nov. 1979
⑥ Fired from Henredon, 1/2 Year Sales 7/3/1981
⑦ Retired from Henkel-Harris 12/31/1989

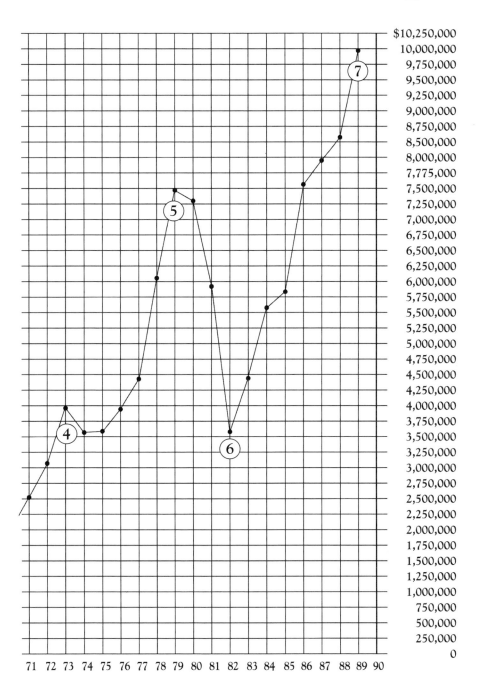

PLATO S. WILSON

May 21, 1982

REJOICE — HELP IS ON THE WAY!

If only General Custer could have heard these words!

Even tho' the skies are cloudy and sales could be better, we have hope for the immediate future — <u>help is on the way</u>! Fortunately, the writer of this letter was a fledgling salesman way back in the '30's. I can remember what we did to "come back" strongly. If you can spare a moment to read my ideas on what we did then and can do now, you will know — <u>help is on the way</u>!

Then, as now, we had a buyer's market. What a challenge to be our best! Anyone can lay down and play dead — but the fun is in the knowledge <u>you can cope</u>. And, you can — if you really want to! Statistics show that the best persons only use 30% of their potential — the average only 20%! These leave a lot of reserve in each of us. So, with this in mind, let's see how we can use — "the help that is on the way."

First of all, we have to have confidence in <u>ourselves</u> and our national economy. We have a real strong leader in Ronald Reagan at the top. He should inspire our confidence. His job is not easy nor is ours. Our interest rates will come down when our Congress finally discovers our future is at stake. This will happen soon. It has to!

In the meantime, we, by ourselves, have many things to do. We must stay positive each day and deliver our best efforts. This is something new for most of us. We have all been spoiled with our lush markets for so long. We have to return to the basics and do them well.

In the 1930s we did our best each day with these tools:

(1) Be inspired by your company!
(2) Keep open your imagination of new ways to sell!
(3) Take the product to your clients! Don't wait for them to come to you.
(4) Think how big the market is and how little I am getting of it.
(5) Project ways to communicate with potential customers!
    (a) Write friendly letters to past clients.
    (b) Call old customers and see how their past purchases are doing.
    (c) Send out store brochures that sell your store!
    (d) Secure names of potential customers that you could contact — and do.

---

(6) When you are with a customer:
- (a) Be organized and professional and at your best.
- (b) Have a real reverence for that customer and her money.
- (c) Do what it takes to make the customer want to buy from you — which means doing all the little things that others will not do for them.
- (d) Ask the customer a lot of questions — you can learn so much — then the customer is more a part of the selling experience!
- (e) Relax your customer — they are up-tight!
- (f) Be genuinely excited — your mood is contagious!

(7) Ask your last customer for prospects for the future. They will do it gladly — a relative, a neighbor, a friend. Then you've got an army working for you! It works for the routine doing.

(8) Call or write your customer after furniture has been delivered. This shows the client you are genuinely interested in them. They will buy more from you!

(9) Keep good records for each client for future use!

(10) Don't let success go to your head! Remember — "you are as good as your last day's performance"! Believe me! Nothing succeeds like repeated success!

The above suggestions are just a few basic ones. You can add to this growing list. As you can see, your job as a professional creative salesman can be so exciting. Doing all this makes you even more excited in your chosen profession. Also, note, "the help that is on the way" comes mostly from you! You can be so helpful to yourself if you only try — and discover this fact. I have a quote that I think of daily — it is by Henry Wadsworth Longfellow: "Not in the clamor of the crowded street, not in the shouts and plaudits of the throng, but in ourselves, are triumph and defeat." Summer is fast approaching! As you all know — this is our best selling season in our area. There will be many people visiting our great state on vacation and buying trips. This is a good time to be at our sharpest performance. Give this important season your very best shot. Your success will become a permanent part of your future career! I'm excited as I know you are. Let's all be something more than we are now!

Please know that you have many friends in this industry that think you are very important. The way you do your daily work with excitement will be a compliment to us all. Plato Wilson will especially be grateful and happy if you become the best salesperson that you can possibly be. I will be watching you carefully and will be standing by to help you. <u>DARE TO BE EXCELLENT</u>! You can do it if you simply have the desire and will to pay the price. I know you will!

Respectfully submitted,

Plato Wilson

Henredon
fine furniture

PLATO S. WILSON

April 11, 1980

SPRING SALES SEMINAR

We have always been convinced that the "last two feet" of the long chain from manufacturing to the home are the most important. These "two feet" are the feet of the retail consultant who makes the sale. All is in vain if the message there is not told effectively.

The task of keeping up-to-date information before your selling people is a difficult one. Many hours of our time are spent with these people, but we have not done an effective job.

Our suggested solution is in the form of an offer. We propose to have the best one-day sales meeting ever held at a factory with complete instructions for you and your selling personnel. We feel that when the people leave our High Point showroom and factory that they will be much closer to HENREDON and the furniture industry. The professional meeting will breed confidence to your people which can be translated to your customer in the form of additional orders. We can do here in a day what it would take us months to do less effectively in your store.

This is how the program will be conducted: We will hold two identical meetings so that more of your personnel can attend. The first date will be Monday, May 12 and the second will be Wednesday, May 14.

We thought Sunday and Tuesday could be used for travel time for personnel from more distant areas. Our meeting will begin in the High Point showroom on the two dates at 9 A.M. sharp and last all day, with lunch being served in our showroom. At the close of each day we plan a cocktail party and dinner. The dinner will be over about 9:00 P.M., allowing a return home of personnel closer by.

We at HENREDON will be host for the day. You, as our customer, will sponsor the travel to and from High Point. We will provide accommodations for overnight, if they are desired. Enclosed you will find a confirmation sheet that is to be filled out <u>promptly</u> by you and returned to me so final arrangements can be made.

This appears to be a wonderful opportunity for us to help our invaluable selling people do a better job. This is not our first venture into a meeting of this type, and we are most enthusiastic about what we can accomplish with your full cooperation. So, get busy <u>today</u> and send us as many people as possible and come yourself!

Cordially yours,

Plato S. Wilson
Salesman

Success is – doing all the little things that an ordinary person chooses not to do!

HENKEL-HARRIS

COMPANY, INCORPORATED
Manufacturers of Fine Furniture

PLATO S. WILSON

November 6, 1989

To My Best Friends: <u>My Retail Customers</u> and <u>Their Staffs</u>!

By now, I'm sure the word has reached you that I plan to retire as of December 31, 1989. What a career I have had with you! The attached letter of resignation from Henkel-Harris captures a lot of my feelings at this time.

This letter is a cover focus of how I feel towards my closet friends — you in the retail business where I spent every working day of my 44 years. They call us "Factory Men" — but in reality, we truly are "Retail People"! The real battles and victories are at the front lines — in the Retail Stores! That's where the battles are won and lost! Thank all of you for helping me to win most of them for my factories and for you!

The event that brought on my decision to retire one year early was my pending re-marriage in January 1990. Fortunately for me, I have found the "perfect lady" to spend the rest of my days with. We will live in High Point — so I will not totally depart the furniture world!

Saying good-bye to good friends is very tough. You all have made a most wonderful life for me. You have always made each and every visit enjoyable and rewarding for me. I truly love each of you; let me try to count the ways: your understanding, cordialness, warmth, sense of humor, hospitality, patience, willingness, courage, truthfulness,

---

honesty, acceptance, listening — and yes, our spirited discussions — all have constantly endeared you to me. Thank you! I have a very long memory and shall never forget you! You have made me more than I deserve to be!

I plan to make one last visit to each of your fine stores before the end of the year to tell you personally how I feel. Somehow, my desires are to propel you into the 90s in a fashion that is fitting for you. So, until I see you for the last time, I hope you continue to have good business for the balance of this year and onward!

My Best Always,

Plato S. Wilson
Sales Representative

Success is – doing all the little things that an ordinary person chooses not to do!

October 14, 1981

To My Former Customers: This has been a long hot summer! I have been waiting since July 6th to write this letter to you. HENKEL-HARRIS has seen fit to appoint me to be their representative for North Carolina and South Carolina effective at the October market. You can't imagine how happy I am with this good news. They were my first choice from the beginning!

HENKEL-HARRIS, as you well know, makes the finest 17th and 18th Century reproductions in America. Quality is a very rare thing these days — but they persevere. Their enlarged facilities will enable more people to enjoy this great product. Their distribution is now being studied, and I will be in a position to discuss this with you at the market.

I hope you have not forgotten me and that you will find me in the HENKEL-HARRIS space which is located on the 1st floor of the main building of the Southern Market Center. I have purchased two new pairs of shoes for the event — so you can recognize me!

We have made beautiful music in the past, and I trust we can "Play It Again" with the HENKEL-HARRIS line whose trademark is: "Just Possibly... America's Finest Furniture." Isn't it funny how lines come and go? I know this is the finest made, and I want to discuss with you the possibility of you becoming more familiar with this exceptional line of furniture.

"Ole Casey" now has another time at bat! Come see the results!

Cordially,

Plato S. Wilson

To: Graduate School, High Point College 3/31/87

HOW TO APPLY AND EXECUTE A JOB IN THE FURNITURE INDUSTRY

I JOB DESCRIPTION

(1) You represent the factory — often the only representative!

(2) Responsibility

    (a) Single your company out for its "unique difference".

    (b) Gain best possible floor placement (space).

    (c) Obtain orders sufficient to support the factory.

    (d) Handle complaints fast and satisfactorily.

    (e) Be aware of dealer credit rating.

(3) <u>Qualifications</u>

    (a) Like people and use good manners

    (b) Honesty and grace

    (c) Self starter

    (d) Highly motivated

    (e) Able to handle rejection and success

    (f) Perseverance

    (g) Ability to wear well

    (h) Good business judgment

    (i) Use of a business education (administration, tax, economic efficiency)

    (j) a problem solver

II APPLYING FOR THE JOB

(1) Apply to as many factories as possible.

(2) Have a professional resume.

(3) Prepare an excellent cover letter.

(4) Dwell on how you can make the company money.

(5) Be punctual on interviews.

(6) Dress your best – shine your shoes – have a smile on your face.

(7) Ask a lot of questions.

III AFTER GETTING THE JOB

(1) Familiarize yourself with accounts.

(2) Ask for a factory man to go with you around territory — if possible.

(3) Organize territory in cloverleaf and try to visit accounts each 6 weeks.

(4) Time is all you have — use it wisely.

IV MAKING A CALL

(1) Write a card to advise dealer you are coming / make advance motel reservations.

(2) Call on accounts 9 a.m. to 4 p.m. (drive to the next town that night).

(3) Try to be fresh — always neat and polite.

(4) Spend time with all individuals (even warehouse and delivery men).

(5) Be efficient but never in a hurry (never just "hang around").

(6) Leave them happy.

V THE SALE

(1) You have to make three sales (on three different calls).

(a) The product

(b) The display

(c) Motivating store personnel to sell product.

VI UNDERSTAND PURPOSE OF A SALESMAN

(1) To be an extension of the factory

(2) Salesmanship:

(a) The capacity to get people to act.

(b) The ability to persuade other persons to support an idea willingly and happily.

(3) To move the product from the factory to the home.

(4) Like a plumber — keep the pipelines open — not clogged!

(5) Establish constant good will.

VII "PROS" AND "CONS"

"Pros"

(1) Nice clean job.

(2) A chance to use 100% of your abilities

(3) Much room for advancement

(4) You are your own boss

(5) Success is rewarding

"Cons"

(1) Very hard work.

(2) Away from home much of time.

(3) Rejection.

(4) Rigid schedules.

(5) Expenses before payments.

VIII WHO ARE SALESMEN? (Some are not!)

IF YOU -

(1) Love people.

(2) Are highly motivated.

(3) Optimistic.

(4) Problem solver.

(5) A self-starter.

(6) If you marry a wife who will let you travel five-day weeks.

(7) Don't mind traveling a lot.

(8) Put other people first.

(9) Not easily discouraged.

(10) If you can't do anything else in life!

- - - - - **you will be a very successful salesman!!**

Plato S. Wilson

MORGANTON HIGH SCHOOL
57ᵀᴴ REUNION – CLASS OF 1943
"OUR MILLENNIUM REUNION"
"THE CAT'S TALE CONTINUES"

Dear Classmates,

On Saturday night at 12:01, 2000, our new millennium began — and with it, The Class of '43 celebrated, each in their own way and location! What a victory to have lived in two millenniums! Knowing our class, I'm sure we refuse to look like it! The heralded Class of '43 can handle anything! Well, almost anything! Can you possibly believe your committee is talking about yet another bigger and better reunion? You will fondly remember our 40th ('83), 45th ('88), 50th ('93) - and now our "MILLENNIUM 57th". Heck, we don't even look 57 and certainly don't act it! What an extraordinary class we are! Forever young!!

From our past attendance, I feel that this class just loves to get together and visit. And that is exactly what we should do for the New Millennium! Don't you agree? Your "committee" met this last summer and has come up with a most appropriate event for this celebration. The following is what to expect:

Saturday, May 6, 2000: 5:00 - 7:00 p.m.

Social Time and Picture Taking at the Morganton Community House, 120 N. King Street

(Picture at 6:30 sharp!)

7:00 p.m. - 'Til

Delicious dinner at the Community House followed by, hopefully, an entertaining program. Afterwards, if you wish, dance to Digital Music as long as you can!

To be sure, we'll be eating, listening to tall tales, reminiscing, dancing and having our usual good time being young again! We have chosen, not one but, two themes for this special "bash" — "Our Millennium Reunion" and "The Cat's Tale Continues." And, those "cats" that graduated in '43 have some great tales to tell! Believe me!! We are not like the tongue-tied ice fisherman who said, "My tale is told!"

As we have done in the past, we plan another up-to-date class directory printed and presented at the reunion. Will you please complete the reservation sheet attached. You can return this to Bill Connelly, 216 Camelot, Morganton, NC 28655 along with your check made out to Bill Connelly — $20 per attendee. If you cannot possibly attend, please send in the information sheet anyway, and we'll send you a directory by mail. In the past, this directory has been most useful and appreciated by all. We would like to have all this information back to us **no later than March 15th** so we can make all arrangements and have them confirmed.

You all had such a grand time at our past reunions, so I know you will not want to miss this "millennium" one! Any reunion after our 50th one is very special indeed — just to show up and say, "Here I am!" Our plans are well underway and <u>they</u> <u>certainly</u> <u>include</u> <u>you</u>! Classmates already contacted are most enthusiastic, so it promises to be another super occasion to be remembered. Do not put this letter down until you have, <u>this</u> <u>day</u>, made your plans to come! I know you will not want to miss this "Millennium Splash" — champagne and all!

So, drop everything, examine your traveling bag for one more trip, tell your kids and grandkids that you are "out of here" for your 57th, gas up the family car and head for home, Morganton, North Carolina, for the event of the year, May 6, 2000! After all, how many invitations do you receive to go to a "Millennium Reunion -57"? Please do not disappoint us, for we can't wait to see you!

Fondly,

Plato S. Wilson
For the committee
2/10/00

A-26

3/27/95   #40
TO: LITTLE BOOGER BAND
RE: GIGS PLANNED

<u>NEW GIGS:</u>

<u>May 13, 1995 Saturday Night:</u> I believe I have talked with all of you about this third Gig for May. It has agreed to do this. This is a "Pool Soiree" and is being organized by Jean Herring and Betsy Collins for their club Soiree! It will be held pool side of the HP Country Club from 6:30 - 9:30 PM. We will eat with them! WE should dress in Summer Uniform (White shorts, flowered shirt and tennis shoes.) This should be much fun! (Pay $400.00) My wife has told me that I cannot be there since she was surprising me with a book club to Delaware on this date. I am very sorry, but Jack can fill in for me, I'm sure!

<u>May 22, 1995 Monday Night:</u> The Salvation Army, which I am its chairman, is launching a tremendous $5 Million Endowment Campaign with this dinner meeting featuring Tom Haggai as guest speaker. It will be at Green St. Baptist Church on Rotary Drive from 5:50 - 8:00 PM. We play in the beginning and then afterwards for a program. You are my guest for dinner at approx. 6:30PM. This will, hopefully, be a big event with possibly 400+ in attendance! Regular Dress (Dark pants, white shirts and bow ties).

<u>October 7, 1995 Saturday Night:</u> Mr. Harold Ritch is getting the Class' of '45 & '46 together for their 50th Reunion at the Radisson Hotel in HP. We play for their dance from 8 - 11PM. No food - Regular Dress. They are excited!

Please check your calendars and advise me immediately <u>if you cannot play</u>. I have to confirm.

SUMMARY:

5/13/95 - Pool Soiree, HP Country Club - 6:30 - 9:30P - Food - Summer Dress
5/22/95 - Sal. Army Endow. Dinner - Green St. Baptist - 5:30 - 8:00P - Food - Reg. Dress.
5/27/95 - Debon-Air Dance - T'ville W/With - 8:30 - 11:30P - No Food - Reg. Dress.
9/14/95 - WWII Tankers - Kepley's Barn Hwy 68 - Free BBQ - 6 - 8P - Reg. Dress.
10/7/05 - Class '45 & '46 - Radisson, HP - 8- 11P Dance- No Food - Reg. Dress.
10/14/95 - HP Hardware 100th - Jamestown - 10 - 12 Noon - Reg. Dress.

Thanks, Plato Wilson <u>889-4539</u>.

Copies: Gray Pierce, Wardell, Hauser, Byran, Struss, Cecil and Wilson

"OUR BRIDGE TO THE FUTURE"

(Campaign Name)

Once again, in the spring of 1984, a dilemma faced our church at a time that our church attendance and giving were at low levels. We were faced with these problems:

1. Prospects of maintenance.
2. Remaining downtown or moving to suburbia.
3. Stay downtown and acquire additional land for parking.

A poll was taken after consultation with the Duke University Ministerial Services. The outcome was an overwhelming vote that our mission was to remain downtown. We then proceeded to see just what land was available adjoining our church property and the cost. There was land available across the street, where now stands the Nation's Bank building, but the price seemed very high. We then learned that the Sheraton Hotel parking lot was available (approx. 75 parking spaces) which was owned by Mrs. Delos Hedgecock and available at a rather attractive price of $300,000. At a Charge Conference held after an 11 a.m. service in early 1984, we explained our findings. The church decided overwhelmingly to try to obtain the Hedgecock property. Shortly thereafter, a campaign was formulated under Co-Chairmen Plato Wilson and Doug Lain. Others serving on this steering committee were: Carter Holbrook, Bill Morris Sr., Bill Snotherly, David Dowdy, Robert Rankin, Ann Morris, Mark Pierce, and Bill Green. By May of that year we had the campaign ready for a 1984 kick-off with our former preacher, Bishop Kenneth Goodson, as our motivational speaker on that evening at 7:30.

Our plan was unique in that it worked in reverse of most financial campaigns. Past campaigns had taught us that 80 percent of the amounted needed ($318,250, including carrying interest) would be given by 20 percent of the congregation. We determined what size gifts would be necessary to make this possible. We listed the necessary gifts that would raise the amount of money needed. Example: 1 Gift of $25,000, 1 Gift of $20,000, 1 Gift of $15,000, and so down the list until we reached 50 Gifts of $250. We hoped that various givers would find their appropriate place on the list. In other words, we took the results of earlier campaigns and worked backwards. The results were amazing as to the actual giving response that very closely matched our original expectation. We gave ourselves 14 months in which to raise the $318,250, with our first payment due on 8/1/84 in the amount of $115,000, which we were able to meet on time. On 1/1/85, we paid another $50,000 plus $9,250 in interest (10%). The final payment of the remaining balance plus interest was due on 8/1/85.

The big money came in early in the campaign. Mrs. Delos Hedgecock asked to be able to make the first pledge of $25,000. She was allowed to do so! By 3/25/85 we had 250 pledges in the amount of $249,328, leaving us a balance of $68,922. The official campaign, as scheduled, came to a close on 8/1/85. We had actually raised $280,000, with a shortage of $40,000. We continued on quietly to pare down the remaining indebtedness to $28,000.00 We decided not to conflict with our every-member canvas for the church budget, that we should finance this amount and pay off as we received additional funds for this project. The last payment was made in August 1986. There was a small "note burning" held in September 1986 on the site of the newly acquired parking lot.

This was done with the leadership of the following ministers:

Rev. Patrick Heafner   Until 6/85
Rev. Linwood Brooks
Rev. Milford Thumm   From 6/85 to 6/87
Rev. Ron Robinson
Rev. Earnest Price

I think that our church turned itself around, with much help from God, by proving to ourselves that we could do important things to preserve our great church in downtown High Point. The next event was a gift of Bishop Bevel Jones who sent us a reward by allowing the Rev. Howard Allred to come and continue our progress. This was in June of 1987. Dr. Allred became the dynamic person and preacher needed to enrich our faith and feed our souls. Truly, the acquiring of the additional parking lot and the experience of Howard Allred were indeed "Our bridge to the future"!

We at First United Methodist will be forever grateful for all of its members who stepped up and made those sacrificial gifts enabling us to secure the parking lot at a time when our need was greatest! Thank you most sincerely! Thanks, also, to Howard Allred who re-established our future!

Plato S. Wilson
908 Parkwood Cir.
High Point, NC 27262

THE GREATER HIGH POINT AREA SALVATION ARMY ENDOWMENT FUND

A statement from Plato Wilson, chairman of the Advisory Board and Endowment.

"With reductions in future federal, state and local grants, we at The Salvation Army here in High Point feel that we must look ahead for a more consistent and stable source of income. For a year now, we have been planning to launch a Home Town Salvation Army Endowment whereby the wonderful people in the Greater High Point Area can contribute to an Endowment. This can be accomplished by giving cash, stocks, bonds, real estate, etc. A second phase will be the use of Wills, Charitable Remainder Trusts, Insurance, etc. This Endowment, as it grows, will make the future of The Salvation Army be assured for present and future helpful programs. The Endowment Fund will be forever for the exclusive use of The Greater High Point Area. The beautiful part of an Endowment is that it gives and gives and the principal is never used up!

We are very proud of the Educational portion of our campaign, just completed on 4/19/95, in the form of an Educational Conrad Teitell Seminar. This noted speaker on charitable giving brought Professionals (CPA's, Lawyers, etc) together for a morning session and the Public for the afternoon session. The attendance was excellent! Results have already become evident!

We now look towards the next phase of the campaign, our Annual Meeting and Formal Launching of the Endowment Campaign. This will be held on 5/22/95 at the Green Street Baptist Church at 6:00 p.m. We are indeed honored to have that great salvationist, Mr. Tom Haggai, as our inspiring speaker! The meal should be excellent, and there will be other stirring entertainment, as well! Tickets, for $10, are available at The Salvation Army office at 301 W. Green St. (883-2769). We look forward to seeing you there!"

Plato S. Wilson

Notes

Notes

Notes

Notes

Notes